Amongst other t̄hings, Fountain has worked as a Civil Servant, a painter and decorator, a woodturner, an assembler of Ford tractors, a lorry driver and a maker of barrage balloons. The first thing he wrote professionally was a short story for BBC national radio (1978). Since then he has written four radio dramas for Radio Telefis Eireann (Irish national radio) and several stage plays. He has an MA in Playwriting Studies from Birmingham University. His interests include music, motorcycling, painting, printmaking and photography.

SOME KIND OF ARTIST

David Fountain

First published in 2018

© Copyright David Fountain 2018

The moral right of David Fountain to be identified as the author of this work has been asserted by him in accordance with the Copyright Designs and Patents Act 1988.

All rights reserved. No part of this publication may be reproduced or transmitted in any form or by any means, electronic or mechanical, including photocopying, recording or any information storage or retrieval system, without either prior permission in writing from the publisher or a license permitting restricted use in the United Kingdom. Such licenses are issued by the Copyright Licensing Agency, 90 Tottenham Court Road, London W1P 0LP.

All photographs © Copyright David Fountain 2018.

Cover design © Copyright David Fountain 2018.

The author can be contacted by email to:-
davidjohnelroro@gmail.com

Art is long, and Time is fleeting

Henry Longfellow

Some Kind of Artist

I got back from college filled with a new energy, took the lift to the tenth floor, went out on the balcony and watched the setting winter sun paint the clouds like a watercolour. I wrote a little poem about it. It was my first tentative, faltering artistic creation.

That new energy inside me was tumultuous and needed bleeding off, needed expression. I'd just turned twenty at the time and little did I know that it would be many years of struggle before I would be able to successfully use that powerful creative force, or that I would have a really bad time of it before things came sort of right.

I was in Stoke-on-Trent near the end of the first term of a Business Studies Higher National Diploma. I'm still slightly amazed that I came to be there at all – studying aspects of business is about as far away as possible from things that interest me now, from my true self.

Many years after that college course at the North Staffordshire Polytechnic I studied art, wrote several radio dramas and a short story which were broadcast by the BBC and RTE (Irish National radio), and in the 1990's when I was in my late forties I gained a Master of Arts degree in Playwriting Studies from Birmingham University. I've come a long way since those days at Stoke and it's been a rocky road.

*　　　　　　　　　*　　　　　　　　　*

The first school I remember anything about really is Chalkwell Hall Junior School in Leigh-on-Sea (or possibly Westcliff – it's very near the boundary).

I went to Chalkwell Hall because of a bus conductor. One day just after we'd moved to Leigh-on-Sea I was on a bus to Southend with my mum and she asked the conductor which was the nearest school to Recreation Avenue where we lived. The conductor told Mum that Chalkwell Hall was much nearer than Westleigh Schools, the other contender, so that's where I ended up going.

Chalkwell Hall school was built in 1909 from red brick.

I suppose I was about three or four when this was taken. That's my mum in the background on the right. Not sure who the other woman is.

The Headmaster during the time I was there was Mr Baggs, a very tall, slender gentleman who was always smartly dressed in a dark suit and wore glasses with thick black frames.

Me at Joss Bay 1953 when I would have been nearly two. I'm wearing a yellow knitted costume, the height of fashion in those days but it was very impractical when wet because it sponged up the water, became very droopy and weighed a ton!

I have a memory of walking past an upstairs classroom with an open door and seeing a little girl sitting on the lap of the teacher as he sat at his high desk at the front of the class. The sight of it disturbed me but I didn't know why. Many years later I saw in the local paper that the same teacher had been prosecuted and jailed for molesting children.

I guess I was about five when this was taken in the mid-fifties. A ghost seems to have stolen the top of my sister's head. My mum must have been having driving lessons at the time. She passed at her second attempt some thirty or forty years later. The car is a 1938 or 1939 Hillman Minx.

Anthony, a good friend of mine at the time, was crossing the playground and walked in front of a girl being swung round by the hands by another girl. Poor Anthony had both his legs broken by the impact.

The thing I remember most about Anthony is that he loved glove puppets and was made to call his father (a Headmaster) Sir. He later went on to become a doctor and practiced in Africa.

Mum, Dad and Bonnie the dog. Dad was great with picnics. You can see his primus stove and kettle in the background.

Andrew, another friend of mine at the time ran so fast across the playground one day that he broke both his wrists when he held out his hands to stop himself against a brick wall. Years later Andrew's claim to fame was that his older brother Graeme went on to become the lead guitarist in a successful local band called the Kursaal Flyers. Graeme once deliberately winded me while we were playing football in the playground. I thought I was going to die from lack of breath. It was horrible.

A happier memory is of one of the teachers bringing in a record for us to hear as an end of term treat. The record was *Apaché* by The Shadows and I can still remember how the wonderful sound of it filled the hall. I think *Apaché* came out in 1960 when I would have been eight or nine.

I passed my eleven plus and went on to Westcliff High School for Boys, one of the local grammar schools. I was a pretty mediocre student, not excelling at anything. I think my dad had a lot to do with the subjects I chose. He was a very powerful man in a quiet kind of way and I realise now just how much control he had over me. I made many of my choices to satisfy him rather than myself. I'm still very proud of the zero per cent I achieved in an end of term physics exam. My dad was horrified but I was secretly very pleased with myself for having demonstrated in my own way that physics wasn't for me. Nor was chemistry.

Dad came from a very poor background and considered that the best jobs were to be found in offices. I doubt if he'd been in any kind of an office in his life. He'd worked himself up from being an apprenticed car mechanic to a marine engineer. He studied at Dartmouth for his qualifications and served on many different ships including hospital ships in the Second World War. My dad was a brilliant engineer and mechanic.

One of Dad's ships.

When we lived at the Recreation Avenue bungalow (which had four bedrooms) he was often to be found at weekends on the front driveway to the garage fixing cars for workmates.

At the time he worked as a maintenance engineer at the Atomic Weapons Research Establishment (AWRE) on Foulness Island, some miles east of Southend. It's no longer used for that but I believe it still belongs to the Ministry of Defence. It was a very secret place and visitors to the island were severely restricted. In the past huge explosions (simulated nuclear ones) occurred regularly on Foulness Island and the shock waves would travel through the London clay and shake buildings and rattle windows many miles away. These days it's gone quiet. I'm not sure what goes on there now.

Dad often spent the whole weekend fixing his mate's cars on the driveway. I'd often go out there and watch him doing what he did best. Sometimes if he was in a good mood he'd explain how things worked and even let me help him a bit. It's surprising how much I learnt from him over the years and that knowledge still stands me in good stead for fixing things, although these days I hate crawling round under cars, my hands covered in black oil and grease, and I get the garage to do the work.

One of Dad's cars from long ago (I would guess the twenties). That's Ivy, one of Dad's sisters-in-law. I think the little dog might be called Sandy.

Every motorbike or car I ever had until relatively recent years I fixed myself (or with my dad's help and guidance). I'd even tackle quite major jobs like replacing a flywheel starter ring or fitting a new camshaft or pistons. In the old days I often used to decarbonise an engine and grind in the valves. Modern engines don't need that sort of work. He also taught me to respect and look after tools and to always buy good quality ones not the "cheap and nasty" kind which often wear out quickly and break.

The two elderly brothers who shared a house opposite our bungalow and fixed broken radios for a living took exception to my dad's automobile activities and I think complained to the Council and Dad had to stop doing it. My friend Andy from over the road used to call the two old boys Ronnie and Reggie after the Kray twins who were in the news at the time.

One day Dad went over to their house and knocked on the door. It was probably in relation to them having told the Council about him carrying on auto repairs in the front garden. One of them came to the door with a knife in his hand and threatened Dad. The two old fellahs were a bit crazy in some ways and hated any kind of noise (apart from the sound of radios I suppose). Many times I saw one of them come out with shaving foam all over his face to shake his fist at a passing aircraft. (We lived on the flight path of Southend Airport and Bristol Super Freighters heavily laden with cars used to fly low over the bungalow. The thing was though you didn't take any notice of them after a while, but Ronnie and Reggie obviously did).

One time I was given a pair of roller skates with metal wheels and I used to skate up and down the pavement. I must admit, they were rather noisy and must have caused the two old brothers considerable distress. One of them often came out to shake his fist at me.

One of Dad's favourite places was Elmsleigh Engineering where he used to take engines to be re-bored for oversize pistons or cylinder heads to be skimmed. I went with him a few times. It was very much his world in there and I loved the oily smell of the place and the sound of the machines they used which you could hear from the trade counter.

Just up the road from Elmsleigh Engineering was Brown Brothers, a motor factors which sold just about any spare for any car. My dad was often in there either for his own car or someone else's.

*   *   *

At school I loved English Literature but ended up failing the 'A' Level because I couldn't remember any lengthy quotations. Coleridge was one of the poets we studied and the images that formed in my mind on reading some of his work are still strong today (I'm now sixty-five). The green ice cracking and growling in *The Rime of the Ancient Mariner*, the sacred River Alph running through caverns measureless to Man in *Kubla Khan*, the frost performing its secret ministry at midnight. A lot of his images were the product of an imagination made rich by opium and that chimed with me because I was smoking a lot of dope at the time.

I was nineteen when this picture was taken. The bike is my beautiful Norton Dominator 600 on which I used to ride to school.

I wasn't particularly good at school subjects but nonetheless I loved the school itself – it was a safe and cosy haven I went to every day to get away from the domestic strife caused by the breaking down of my parents marriage. I also made many friends there (some very respectable, some complete reprobates) and I liked the eccentricities of many of the masters. I can only remember a couple of female teachers – Mrs Brogden who taught biology and Madame Meyer who taught French.

Mr Brogden (Mrs Brogden's husband) taught Latin and would stand on the low platform at the front of the class and lean forward until he almost fell face down to the floor then would jump forward just in time to save himself.

I did Latin for a year but was pretty hopeless at it.

Mr Hart (I can't remember what he taught, although it may have been French) smelt strongly of perfume as though he'd had a bath in it, and if he passed by the scent lingered for a long time. As you can imagine the kids used to take the micky out of him behind his back.

I remember Mr Dean the geography master who used to spend his lunch breaks making beautiful coloured chalk drawings of physical features on the blackboard which he'd reveal to us when we came into class. At the end of the lesson he'd just wipe away his work of art.

The delightful Mr Lindberg (We called him Spike because of his unusual hair) was tiny and emaciated. He'd survived a Japanese prisoner of war camp in World War Two and taught biology alongside Mrs Brogden. In a big specimen jar he kept a hugely long tapeworm which had been removed from his daughter. Somewhere in the science block there was a place where Spike and Mrs Brogden bred various creatures for dissection by students. I remember frogs, rats and dogfish (although I daresay the dogfish were bought already dead). I also remember tiny, perfectly formed frogs which had been given some chemical or other (I think it was formaldehyde) which had dramatically stunted their growth. I remember being rather sickened by the smell of a dissected dogfish and alarmed at having to cut open a rat and pin its skin to a board, thereby exposing its internal organs.

Another favourite teacher was a young guy fresh from college who arrived every day on an ancient motorcycle combination. He taught chemistry and if a boy had a headache he'd mix up some chemical concoction in a beaker and give it to the kid to drink.

I never did art at school and I think the main reason for that was that my dad was very distrustful of the Arts (although he loved classical music and was a choirboy when he was young) and he would have steered me towards subjects he considered useful. If he'd have had his way my sister would not have been allowed to go to art college, but a combination of my mum overruling him and my sister's tenacity and strength of character put paid to any ideas he might have had in that direction.

Outside the art room was where we smoked. It was hidden away at one end of the building near some bicycle sheds and you were unlikely to be discovered.

I started smoking when I was fourteen. Every year Devonshire Grandma (my dad's mum) would send us a Christmas parcel with presents for all the family. Inside there was always a box of 100 *Senior Service* untipped cigarettes and it lay pretty much untouched for weeks on top of the piano in the front room (a sort of parlour only really used at Christmas and when my mum fancied playing the piano) because my dad didn't like them very much and my mum only smoked *Du Maurier* cigarettes (one red box of twenty every Christmas as a special treat to herself!) Dad rolled his own cigarettes from *Golden Virginia*. He had a horrible habit of opening up the dog ends and putting the stinking, tarry tobacco back in his tin. Every so often I'd take a cigarette from the box on the piano and smoke it in the garden. I soon got hooked and started buying packets of twenty *Nelson*, *Sovereign* or *Number 6*. My addiction lasted until I gave up when I was fifty-two. I was returning from visiting my friend Liz in Canterbury in the Renault camper van I had at the time. I'd rolled three or four cigarettes for the journey home and was halfway through the first when I decided I didn't want to be a slave to tobacco any more. I threw the rest of the cigarette out the window and haven't smoked since. I still get occasional pangs even after thirteen years and I know I'd only need one cigarette to be back on them again.

Tod, Steven and Mike were three of my reprobate friends from school and we used to get up to all sorts of mischief in the evenings and at weekends.

One evening we were up to mischief down by the Fenchurch Street railway line near Chalkwell Station where there's an embankment. We got over the fence and were messing about at the bottom of the embankment. I discovered a thick, black electrical cable pretty well buried in the undergrowth. I had a wooden-handled knife with a foldaway blade in my pocket and I proceeded to hack through the cable (to this day I don't know why I did it) until a big flash and bang startled me enough to jump back. The four of us ran away from the crime scene pretty quickly.

It turned out I'd cut through the power supply cable to the emergency signalling system which ran the forty or so miles from Fenchurch street to Shoeburyness, the end of the line. I learnt this when two British Rail policemen came knocking a few days later.

Someone in a nearby house had seen us running away and recognised Mike who lived very near Chalkwell Station. They'd told the railway police and he grassed up the other three of us! I didn't hold it against him really though because I expect they put a lot of pressure on him in the presence of his parents. We were only fourteen at the time and were let off with a stern caution (plus a severe telling off from our parents).

All in all I'm lucky to be alive considering some of the stupid and dangerous things I got up to when young.

Another close call I had was one day when my dad was showing me how to make something in the garage. He had a very ancient electric drill with a metal casing. Dad passed it to me and when I pressed the trigger a mains voltage electric shock went up my right arm. I remember it being like a deep and powerful vibration. I wasn't able to release the trigger. My dad realised I was being electrocuted and turned it off at the plug. His quick action certainly saved my life. Another second or two and my heart could have stopped. Dad was very shocked by what had happened and told me it was probably best not to tell Mum, so I didn't.

October was a good time for us because that's when fireworks became available. One of our favourite tricks was letting off rockets on the seafront. We used to lay them on the ground, light the touch paper and watch them shoot away along the promenade just above ground level. It was amazing how far and fast they travelled.

Bangers were good because of the gunpowder they contained. If you cut a few of them in half you could get a nice little pile of the stuff.

I remember one time I made a rudimentary gun. I flattened one end of a piece of copper pipe and held it in my dad's big engineering vice. I found a bolt that was a pretty snug fit in the open end of the pipe. I lit a banger and while it was fizzing quickly inserted it into the pipe and just had time to insert the bolt before a huge explosion sent it the length of the garage and embedded it in one of the wooden doors.

Another time I did something incredibly stupid and dangerous in my bedroom. I opened the window then put a fizzing banger in an empty glass coffee jar and screwed on the metal lid. I just had time to place the jar on the window sill outside the non-opening window and retreat inside the room before a huge explosion shattered the jar into fragments and made me deaf for a day or so. I can't imagine what the neighbours must have thought but no doubt they were used to explosions being caused by the strange boy next door!

On another occasion the four of us found an old tree stump at the edge of a field and we made a rudimentary bomb from weedkiller and sugar and blew the stump to bits (I can't remember how we detonated it). That was good fun if a trifle dangerous.

*   *   *

I'm in my cot. My mum comes in to pull the curtains and tuck me in. She climbs on to the brown polished dressing table to pull the curtains but slips and her shin scrapes down the top corner of the dressing table. I realise she's badly hurt. She goes out of the bedroom which is my parent's bedroom at the front of the flat. I think Nanna and Grandpa live upstairs. This is probably the same house where I fell down the stairs. My next memory of the event is of Mum sitting in an armchair with her injured and dressed leg propped up on a cushion on a box or something similar. I think she spent several days like that. It must have been a nasty and painful injury.

My mum in 1948, a few years before I was born.

Now I'm four or five years old, sitting on a pillow at the head of my parent's bed. It's the same room. It's a bright, sunny day and light pours in through the big bay window. I'm aware that my mum is in another part of the house. A radio is playing loudly. The song *Green Door* comes on and I'm fascinated by the lyric and sound of the song. It's my first memory of music.

All my life music has played a huge part.

From the late 1950's my sister, who's a few years older than me, bought rock 'n' roll singles with her pocket money. I think they were 6/8d each, which meant you could get three for exactly a pound. Most weeks on a Saturday she'd go to the record store and come home to play her new acquisitions on her red record player. I used to love hearing that fantastic music whenever she was at home. Elvis Presley singing *Jailhouse Rock, It's Now or Never* or *His Latest Flame.* I still love early Elvis Presley. That music has such exciting, raw power. One day she came home with an Eddie Cochran album (I imagine it would have been soon after he died) and that music blew me away (although being me I probably kept it to myself). Sometimes she'd have one or two friends round and they'd jive away in the living room.

My sister Tina directing my pedal car.

Next door lived a retired policeman and his wife and their daughter was about the same age as my sister. One time in the early 1960's she bought *The Three Bells* by the Browns and played it loudly and incessantly – maybe ten times in a row, time after time. Our bungalow was semi-detached and the two living rooms backed onto each other. The wonderful sound of that song travelled through the brick wall so loudly you could make out the lyric. I still love *The Three Bells* whenever I hear it.

One of the first bands I saw live was Frank Zappa and the Mothers of Invention. They were playing at the Albert Hall and I went up there on the train with Tod (who took his own life in his early thirties). Tod was quite bizarre in many ways and that extended to his choices in music. The band was fantastic. As we approached the Albert Hall a couple of band members were hanging around outside smoking and chatting.

Frank Zappa himself was a wonderful performer (and a great lead guitarist) and the spaces between the numbers were filled with his wacky sense of humour. At one point Motorhead (their keyboard player) made his way through the audience to the big church-type organ and played some amazing stuff. It seemed impromptu but I guess it must have been arranged.

At school my best friend was Pete Lee. It was him who introduced me to music in a big way. Pete was short and slight with long, straight black hair. He always dressed in black (apart from his dark blue school blazer which was compulsory). Pete was very much the black sheep of his family. His father was a headmaster in a junior school, his older brother was a teacher and his mum was a Sunday school teacher. Pete disliked school and was out of there as soon as the 'O' Levels were over (I don't think he got any – he never did any school work).

Pete lived for music. He had taught himself electric lead guitar and he was very accomplished. Had he not succumbed to drugs in a big way I'm sure he could have been a very fine blues guitarist.

Blues was his thing and it became my main musical interest too. There was a sadness within Pete and myself which drew both of us to the music of the American slaves.

Pete was obsessed and by association I became obsessed too. The very first record I bought was *Rhythm and Blues All Stars* published by Marble Arch. It had tracks by Howlin' Wolf, Muddy Waters, Buddy Guy and many other fine blues men. It's still one of my favourite albums.

Pete had a talent for seeking out what was the best in blues and steering me in that direction.

There used to be a department store in central Southend called Dixons and they always had bargain bins. One day Pete tipped me off about a brilliant 45 single he'd seen for next to nothing in one of the bins. I was down there like a shot and bought the last copy. It was *Goin' Down Slow* by Howlin' Wolf. I don't know what happened to it – maybe got lost in a move – but I remember it had a green cover with a photo of an empty rocking chair.

Pete and I had many musical adventures. Several times we went to the Hammersmith Odeon to see the American Folk Blues Festivals that were put on there from 1967. I would have been sixteen or seventeen at the time. We saw some of the blues greats such as John Lee Hooker and the astonishing harmonica player Big Walter Horton. We always sat as close to the stage as possible and I remember looking up at Walter Horton in a spotlight and being mesmerised by the brilliance of his playing. We saw Howlin' Wolf and Muddy Waters at one point but I can't remember where.

It's possible that Pete's ancestry included Romany gypsies – his surname Lee was certainly that of one of the big gypsy clans. A kind of shared ancestry (some of my ancestors on my mum's side were Lees) was maybe one reason we got on so well.

There's a pub in Southend called The Cricketers (it's still a good music pub) and back in the mid-sixties they started putting on mostly white blues bands on Friday nights. It had a smoky, sleazy atmosphere, perfect for a blues club and there was a little bar in the corner and people sitting on the stairs up to the toilets. We were far too young to get served but neither Pete nor I were interested in alcohol anyway – we preferred to smoke a joint before listening to a band.

Of course Pete and I went down there whenever we could and sat close to the small stage, which was only raised a few inches, and absorbed some fantastic music. We saw Chicken Shack with the amazing Stan Webb on guitar and Christine Perfect on piano (who later became Christine McVie of the second incarnation of Fleetwood Mac), Ten Years After, The Crazy World of Arthur Brown (who used to set his Viking helmet on fire. Wouldn't be surprised if he still does), Black Cat Bones, Freddie King and so many others, but the band that stood out way above the others as far as Pete and I were concerned was the original Fleetwood Mac … Peter Green's Fleetwood Mac as they were known in those days. That was when they were a brilliant blues band and Peter Green was one of the finest blues guitarists that ever lived (he's still alive but doesn't play so much these days). He was a very impressive-looking guy with his long dark hair and good looks. Also in the band was Jeremy Spencer who played slide guitar often in the style of Elmore James, John McVie on bass and Mick Fleetwood on drums. The last two went on to form the rejuvenated Fleetwood Mac (which is still going strong as far as I know) after Peter Green left the band in 1970 because he couldn't handle the fame. All he wanted to do was play the blues – he didn't want fame and it all got a bit out of control for him.

Pete and I saw them in 1967 when they were at the height of their powers. We sat right by the stage just a few feet away from the band.

That music cut deep into our souls. Peter Green's guitar solos were beautiful beyond belief. The notes flew like sparse scatterings of birds, hovered round the room or went deep down in the ground. In all my years I've never been more affected by a band than I was that night.

Pete's home life came to an abrupt end when the Drug Squad raided the family home one evening. Pete's room was in the attic and his parents were unaware that it had become a regular little drug den with all sorts of undesirables trooping up the stairs every evening to have fun with cannabis and LSD (and possibly harder things too). The house was watched and when the maximum number of people was there the Drug Squad struck. Fortunately for me I wasn't there at the time.

Following his conviction Pete was sent to a young offenders place in Kent for a good few months.

His parents told him he was no longer welcome home and after his release he camped out at various friends' places and got into drug taking in a big way.

I didn't see much of him any more because I could see where it was heading and I didn't want to be near stuff like that. He still remained a good friend though and I saw him from time to time.

*   *   *

It's the autumn of 1969. I'm seventeen. I've been out for the evening and now I'm standing in the garden smoking a little joint. The moon's almost full and the air is cold and it feels like there might be a frost later. It's a weekday and my dad's in bed. He always gets up early, smokes a few roll-ups, has a couple of cups of tea and goes off to work.

My mum fell in love with the guy next door (not the ex-policeman, that family has gone) and she's moved in with her mum and dad until she can get married so it's just me and my dad. It always feels so awkward, especially when he tries to do domestic things like cooking and hoovering that he's never done before. I feel sorry for him. I feel a great, dark sadness inside me because their marriage fell apart and I so hope that each of them finds a good and happy life.

I go indoors, nicely stoned and put *Electric Ladyland Part Two* by the Jimi Hendrix Experience on my stereo. I let the needle drop onto *Voodoo Chile* and listen through my headphones. I lie on the sofa and close my eyes.

Well the night I was born
I swear the moon turned a fire red.

Jimi sings and plays into my ears, into my brain. As the song plays on the images come alive in my imagination.

Well my arrows are made of desire.

The music is dark and dangerous and feels forbidden somehow. It takes me to places I've never been before.

I taste the honey from a flower named blue.

I suddenly become aware of someone else in the room. I open my eyes and find my dad is standing really close, looking down at me like he's trying to figure something out. I guess he's wondering if his son has been taking drugs. Maybe I had a smile on my face. Whatever it is seems to frighten him. I remove the headphones and he just says quietly, "Isn't it time you were in bed?" and goes out of the room.

*   *   *

It's a Saturday night. I'm in a pub called the *Top Alex* in central Southend. I've taken some LSD. My friends assured me that it's good stuff. Powerful and clean. I took a tablet last Saturday too but it didn't do anything at all so I'm having another go. I want to experience that magic that LSD is supposed to bring. I want sounds to turn into colours and I want pictures in my head of things that aren't there.

Someone buys me a drink and spills some of it on the dark wooden table top. Reflections in the pool of spilt beer become a little world, a brightly coloured planet. The colours shift and change. I'm fascinated by it for what seems like hours but is probably a few minutes.

Eventually my attention comes back to the pub. My friends want to leave. We go outside and in an alleyway I see a luminous pink cat making its way along a fence top.

Nothing much happens after that.

*   *   *

When I was at school I often took a job in the summer holidays.

One place I worked one summer was *The Happidrome*, one of the amusement arcades on Southend seafront (it's still going strong). I worked for Barry who looked after three stalls in there – a darts stall where any treble took a prize, a coconut stall where you had to try and break the orange nylon string supporting the coconuts with air rifle shots (almost impossible to do), and a .22 rifle range which used Winchester and Carbine rifles. This was just for fun and you could shoot at all sorts of things such as metal ducks at the far end of the gallery.

One day I was on the coconut stall and some drunk young men came in and paid for a go on the .22 rifle range (the guns of course used proper bullets). One of the guys turned round and started aiming his gun at people in the arcade. The chain on each gun was long enough to allow this to happen. I ducked down behind my stall. Luckily he didn't shoot anyone before Barry managed to grab the rifle off him.

One day Barry asked me to look after the .22 rifle range while he went to the toilet. He gave me the leather pouch which contained all the bullets and while he was gone I took a few bullets and put them in my pocket.

At home I had an air rifle and one day after school I went in the garden, pointed the rifle in the air and balanced a bullet on the end of the barrel. I then shot a pellet into it and it exploded and a piece of the bullet buried itself in my arm (I still have the scar). It bled profusely and I took myself to the doctor's who told me not to be so stupid in future and the piece of lead would eventually work its way out of my arm. Sure enough a few days later that's what happened.

Another time I worked in the Rossi's ice cream factory which was quite good fun.

*   *   *

The headmaster of Westcliff High was a great guy and known by everyone affectionately as Henry (his real first name). Henry was tall and broad with bushy eye brows and thick set features. He made an impressive sight swanning round the corridors in his black gown and mortar board. He had studied at Cambridge and sometimes taught English.

I took three 'A' Levels – English Literature, Economics and Geography – and only passed Economics with a middling grade.

Henry recommended that I did a correspondence course at home in Geography and put my English Literature fail down to experience. I'd then be able to re-sit Geography at school at the beginning of the next year. In the meantime I was free to do what I wanted as long as I left enough time for working on the correspondence course.

I looked around for jobs and decided to apply to Southend Corporation for a job as a bus conductor. I was interviewed by Derek Giles who ran Southend Corporation Transport. The buses were blue. Mr Giles decided I was a suitable candidate and took me on. He said that, depending how I did as a conductor, I may later decide to apply for driver training.

I loved working as a bus conductor. Working on the buses beat any of the summer holiday jobs hands down. The training included learning how to use your ticket machine and a couple of weeks or so working alongside experienced conductors when you learnt most of the routes, then you were let loose on the public and had to make up any shortfall in your money at the end of the day (conversely you could keep anything over).

Most of the routes were purely urban but the ones I liked best involved a good deal of country work – the number 7's and 8's made their way from Shoeburyness to Rayleigh Station and back again. Much of the journey passed through small rural towns like Rochford, Hawkwell and Hockley and on a weekday late morning or afternoon when there weren't many passengers you could spend a good deal of your time standing on the platform at the back of the bus looking out of the opening and daydreaming as the countryside passed by.

The times I liked the least were early mornings when it was wet and cold and the bus was jammed full of school kids and train commuters and the windows were streaming with condensation and the upper deck was full of cigarette smoke.

You had to learn all the fare stage numbers and when you reached each one you had to adjust your ticket machine so it printed the right number on the tickets.

The bus company owned an old London taxi and if someone didn't turn up for an early morning shift they'd send one of the spare bus drivers round in the taxi to wake them up and get them to work.

My driver was a lovely old fellow called Bill Durrell and we got on extremely well. He was getting near retirement age.

One of our runs terminated at Sutton Road Cemetery and the bus needed turning round and driving the few hundred yards to the bus stop. It was strictly against the rules of course but Bill would sometimes let me get in the cab with him and drive the bus to the bus stop. That was great fun.

*   *   *

One day in 1969 When I was about eighteen my dad dropped a bombshell. He told me out of the blue that he'd be selling the bungalow and moving to Wales so I'd have to move out.

Although it wasn't ideal with just me and my dad, I'd got used to it and it was a shock being told I had to vacate the family home.

Anyway I looked in the local paper and found a bedsit in St Helens Road, Westcliff and moved in there, just taking a few essentials like my busman's uniform, my made-to-measure maroon mohair suit, my stereo and records, some other clothes and other bits and pieces and left everything else behind.

My maternal grandfather, William Bell, was still alive at that time and he'd given me a beautiful old cat's whisker wireless in a mahogany box with ancient headphones. It was something that I imagine had been precious to him and one of the few things he had of any value. My grandparents had at one time been very wealthy but they'd ended up as poor as church mice, living on the state pension and having to worry about how much coal to put on the fire.

That old radio was one of the many things I had to leave behind and I regret to this day that I don't still have it.

Around the time he gave me the wireless he also gave me his gold pocket watch and chain. One night I went out to a disco in my mohair suit and had the watch in a waistcoat pocket with the chain clipped to a buttonhole. Sometime during that night both were stolen from me. I didn't realise till I got home. My mum was so upset about that.

I imagine my dad chucked everything of mine out because I never saw any of it again.

The bedsit was small and depressing but almost as soon as I got there I met the girl from next door who had a big double bedsit and by that evening I'd moved in with her. I had my first sexual experiences with her but we won't go there.

I think this is a good time to introduce some of my relatives and ancestors, seeing as they shaped me and my past and will continue to shape the futures of countless generations to come.

MY MUM'S LOT

Great Grandpa John Fountain – He bought twenty-three acre White's Farm at Aldborough Hatch (near Ilford, now Redbridge, London) on July 15th 1889. The farm cost £1,400. At the same auction a two acre piece of arable land sold for £120.

Great Grandpa John and his Romany wife Ginnie and their four daughters (l to r) Jessie, May, Olive and Kate. Jessie died when she was nineteen.

Over the years Great Grandpa John acquired several roads of little houses for his farm workers. After he died in 1922 the farm and its associated properties was sold for several hundred thousand pounds. The land had valuable gravel underneath which

White's Farm, Aldborough Hatch

was quarried but the farmhouse remained on its own like an island

A circus elephant was kept there when the circus was in town!

in the middle of the gravel pits. It's still there to this day and is now owned by a Korean church.

I think each of his surviving children received £22,000 from the sale – a massive amount those days, equivalent to over a million pounds today. Imagine making each of your ten children millionaires! What a legacy.

```
BRICK-BUILT AND SLATED DWELLING HOUSE
                    CONTAINING
ON THE GROUND FLOOR—Dining Room, Large Drawing Room, with two handsome Marble Mantels, Tiled
    Hearths, and Marble Fenders; Kitchen, with Range, Cupboards, &c., and Pump of Good Water, and Small
    Washhouse; Good Cellar in the Basement.
FIRST FLOOR—Four Bedrooms, with Cupboards.

SURROUNDING THE HOUSE IS A WELL-STOCKED GARDEN.
              THE OUTBUILDINGS
                    COMPRISE
       TIMBER-BUILT AND THATCHED BARN,
           TILED WOOD SHED AND DRILL SHED,
    Thatched Bunching Shed, with Pump and plentiful supply of Water.
   DETACHED TIMBER-BUILT AND TILED GRANARY ON PIERS,
   And a Detached Timber Erection of Cow-house, Stabling for Four Horses, Hen-house,
           and Range of Lofts Over, with enclosed Chicken Run.
    THE WHOLE CONTAINING, AS PER QUANTITIES TAKEN FROM THE ORDNANCE SURVEY,
                 23a.      0r.      25p.,
                       OR THEREABOUTS.
    TOGETHER WITH THE TITHES, BOTH GREAT AND SMALL
           POSSESSION CAN BE HAD ON COMPLETION OF THE PURCHASE
    The Growing Timber, and those Fixtures which belong to the freehold, will be included in the purchase; but the
    Purchaser will have to pay the customary valuation
```

Auction paper from the sale of White's Farm 1922.

Great Grandpa John had his fingers in several pies. As well as owning *Fountains Restaurant* on Southend seafront and a greengrocer's next door (where some of his farm produce was sold), he was also a wrestling promoter. He arranged bouts for famous wrestlers of the time. One such bout was between the Estonian strongman George Hackenschmidt *(The Russian Lion)* and Ahmed Marali *(The Terrible Turk)* who was actually a sixteen stone Frenchman from Marseille. Those were the days when wrestling was a real gentleman's sport.

Fountain's Cyprus Restaurant, Marine Parade, Southend-on-Sea.

Maurice, my mum's brother, told me that his grandfather John used to put up the wrestlers at the farmhouse. Maurice remembered meeting George Hackenschmidt when he was a young boy and the wrestler patted him on the head.

Fountain's greengrocer's, 39-40 Marine Parade, Southend-on-Sea. The Cornucopia pub is to the left of the shop. You can see some beer bottles. The Cyprus Restaurant is to the right of the shop.

Hackenschmidt was the world's first professional heavyweight wrestling champion and was very famous at the time. From his photo you can see he was not a tall man (he was 5' 9") but was squat and very muscular. He reminds me of a tough little dog. He once lifted a small horse off the ground and in 1902 he jumped one hundred times over a table with his feet tied together. Both his Russian father and his Swedish mother were slight in build but his maternal grandfather was said to be massively powerful.

There was huge publicity surrounding the bout between The Russian Lion and The Terrible Turk which took place on 30th January 1904. The match was at Olympia and up to twenty thousand people attended which caused the biggest traffic jam that London had ever known. Traffic was jammed from Olympia back to Piccadilly.

The contest only lasted about two minutes (wrestling matches often went on for hours) before *The Russian Lion* picked up *The Terrible Turk* in a bear hug (a move Hackenschmidt invented) and slammed him to the canvas dislocating his shoulder.

Produce, including peas, from John Fountain's Whites Farm, Aldborough Hatch/Oaks Lane, outside the wholesale fruit and vegetable market in Southwark c.1901. The market workers in the foreground are accompanied by Mr Roberts, a stall holder from Barkingside (wearing a bowler hat). The building in the background is Southwark Cathedral.

The winner's purse was a massive one thousand pounds.

George Hackenschmidt was a very cultured man and spoke seven languages. In later years he wrote many books on physical culture and philosophy. He lived much of his life in London with his French wife and died at ninety in 1968 in South Norwood.

I'm rather proud of the fact that my great grandfather caused London's biggest ever traffic jam.

My sister Tina, who has done a good deal of family research, recently told me that Great Grandpa John's mother had the maiden surname of Lee and was of Romany stock. That being the case, my grandmother Olive was 75% Romany, my mother Eileen half that and Tina and myself about 19% Rom. Until her discovery about Great Grandpa John's mother both Tina and myself had assumed that we were both 12.5% Rom.

So travelling's in our blood. I always thought it must be. I'll have to get a couple of horses and a caravan they can pull along and go on some real adventures! (I'm joking but it would be nice. Not sure where I'd keep the horses though what with living in a second floor flat. Perhaps I could graze it on the public grass area over the road!) Motorcycle adventures, although wonderful, don't quite have the same glamorous appeal as getting around by means of a Gypsy caravan pulled by horses.

Great Grandmother Jane (Ginny) Fountain – A true one hundred per cent Romany gypsy. I imagine White's Farm was on her family's yearly list of places visited for work. It's rumoured that after she married John Fountain she never again left the farm until she died many years later. They had at least five daughters – including Jessie, May, Kate and Olive. Jessie died when she was about 19, as did one of the other daughters, according to my mum. Olive was my grandmother. They also had several sons, all but one I was told died of alcohol abuse.

Olive Fountain (Nanna) – My grandmother, who was born on 18th January 1889. When she was young she was a dark-haired beauty. She was very artistic, as were at least two of her sisters – one was a concert pianist and one was a dancer. Olive's son Maurice (my uncle, 18th December 1916 to 1st August 2007) told me that his mum used to make beautiful painted silk scarves with palm tree motifs which she sold for two or three pounds and which sold on for £70 or £80. He said she was very artistic with flowers and used to make the most beautiful wreaths. Maurice said his mum used to own and run two florists in Hornchurch, one of which was "on the corner of Billington Lane" (although it could possibly have been in Croydon – I could find no trace of a Billington Lane in Hornchurch). He remembered the shops also selling cabbages, beet and swedes and in the autumn turnips and parsnips.

My grandmother, Olive Fountain.

Maurice said he remembered his mum owning a tobacconists in Catherine Street, Croydon "near a billiard hall" (I think that he may have meant Hornchurch. He was a very old man when he told me and may well have got the two places mixed up. He said he was seven or eight at the time (that would make sense - his mum would have recently inherited her fortune). My grandmother also went on to own and run three pubs – The Old Swan in Crediton, Devon (which became Clark's Shoes) another pub in Exmouth.and a third one somewhere else. I remember my mum saying that her

Olive Fountain at White's Farm where she was born. Her sister May is in the background. May died at fiftyish.

mum was often the life and soul of the pub. Grandpa would sit quietly in a corner reading a newspaper and smoking his pipe.

By the time Olive died in 1972 she and my grandfather had long been penniless. When we lived at Motney Hill in Kent when Dad worked at the water treatment works down the road, Nanna and Grandpa lived in a tiny rundown rented cottage (Clark's Cottages) near Pump Lane off the Lower Rainham Road in Rainham. Their cottage was only a mile or so from where we lived. I remember it being a two up, two down. I don't remember there being a bathroom. The two small bedrooms each had a double bed squeezed in and I remember sleeping there with my mum on the odd occasion with a big bolster between us.

Olive and William Richard Bell (Nanna and Grandpa) at Clark's Cottages, Rainham, Kent.

Nanna and Grandpa both painted there and I imagine the cottage always smelled of turpentine, although I don't remember that.

What I do remember is that there was a plastics factory down the road and Nanna used to have vast quantities of plastic ornaments delivered which she used to paint. All I remember now are the white plastic swans lined up like soldiers waiting for Nanna to paint parts of them. It can't have earned them much money but it must have helped relieve their poverty.

After we moved to Southend when I was six or so Nanna and Grandpa followed a while later. One of the bungalows overlooking the garden at Recreation Avenue contained an old lady called Mrs Winn who owned a house in Leigh which had been converted long ago into two flats. Mum arranged with Mrs Winn for Nanna and Grandpa to rent the ground floor flat.

Grandpa with some rather fine cabbages.

I often used to take the rent round to Mrs Winn and she always had a big jigsaw puzzle on the go. She was a friendly old lady and I really liked her. She'd always insist that I complete a couple of pieces of the puzzle before I went home.

Nanna and Grandpa spent the last few years of their lives living in their dingy rented flat in Ronald Hill Grove, Leigh-on-Sea, a few miles from the centre of Southend-on-Sea. Her business skills left a lot to be desired but Nanna and Grandpa were deeply in love until the end and spent their money on having a great life.

Both Nanna and Grandpa painted – Grandpa in watercolour (which seemed to suit his gentleness) and Nanna in oils. I have Grandpa's black metal watercolour boxes which still have some of the original pans of paint going back over a hundred years. I also have an exquisite watercolour sketchbook of his which in a way documents in images his early married life. Nanna was painting almost until she died. One of her last pictures was of birds circling over a moonlit sea.

Watercolour sketch of a tree by William Richard Bell.

Nanna's oil painting of birds circling over a moonlit sea.

Oil painting of WR Bell by Olive Bell (on brass).

Both Nanna and Grandpa used to exhibit their pictures. In Southend they both exhibited in the Beecroft Art Gallery Open Exhibition which started in the early 1960's.

I remember Nanna always used to wear a beautiful thin floral housecoat when she painted in the living room at their small flat. I used to love the smell of turpentine in the room. Whenever I visited Nanna and Grandpa in the winter they'd be huddled by the open fire, Nanna on the sofa, Grandpa in his chair. Nanna and I would play the card game she called Benny (also called Rummy I think) while Grandpa read his book (either a cowboy story or James Bond) and smoked his pipe. The room was really quiet and peaceful. Nanna smoked all her long life – *Player's Weights* which I think were untipped and she had a black cigarette rolling machine which she'd use to roll up her dog ends into new cigarettes. In the past people used to do that. Nanna was rarely without a fag in her mouth and Grandpa always seemed to have his pipe on the go. I remember he used to smoke *Erinmore Flake* which had a very sweet smell. Such lovely memories of lovely people. I so wish now that I'd talked to Nanna and Grandpa about their early lives. It would have been fascinating hearing their stories. Too late now.

As well as Grandpa's watercolour boxes, sketchbook and photo albums I also have his camera which is well over a hundred years old but still in remarkably good condition. Grandpa would have been in his mid-twenties when he bought the camera. As far as I can see the bellows have no holes in them whatsoever and still slide in and out sweetly. The inside of the back cover tells me that the camera is a No. 2 FOLDING POCKET BROWNIE MODEL B and it was manufactured by the EASTMAN KODAK COMPANY of Rochester, New York. The panel then goes on to list the various US patents ranging from January 1902 to September 1909. There's a bit of white paper stuck inside the back panel proclaiming that the camera belongs to W.R. Bell of 60 Windsor Avenue, Hillingdon.

I think this was the only camera that Grandpa ever owned and to me it's really precious, as are his photograph albums which I'm still looking at more than a hundred years after they were made. One of them Grandpa himself made by cutting black pages to size and covering them with a beautiful soft leather cover on which he burnt (using pyrography) a picture of an American Indian in full head dress with the word 'Photographs' alongside it. There's a lot to be said for photograph albums – I wonder in a hundred years time how many of present day people's relatives to come will still be viewing their digital photos. Very few I would think. Most people's photographs will die with them unless they've taken the trouble to make albums out of the best ones.

Grandpa's Folding Pocket Brownie, patented 1909.

I hope that when I'm gone Grandpa's camera, sketch book, photograph albums and watercolour boxes get passed on down the generations. The camera's not worth much because they were made in huge numbers. The engineering is quite exquisite for something so old. The only problem with it is that the shutter is a little sticky, but I daresay that could be put right. It may be because the iris has become slightly corroded over time. Hardly surprising after nearly a hundred and ten years. I wonder how many of today's digital cameras will still be usable in a hundred and ten years? None?!

Grandpa was a really good photographer as is evidenced by his photo albums. He was often very inventive with his viewpoints and undoubtedly saw photography as a novel form of art. Photography was only about seventy years old when he started using his camera.

 Nanna died first (in hospital from bowel cancer). My sister Tina (Christine) told me recently that she apologised for having spent her entire fortune, but admitted she'd enjoyed doing it! Good luck to them is what I say – none of us has any right to expect any money from our relatives when they die – how they choose to spend their money is of course entirely up to them. I remember her being in a single room at the very end. Like all good Rom she requested that her family visit her so she could say goodbye to all those who turned up. I remember going into the room alone and saying goodbye to her as she sat up in bed. It seemed so right to do that. Nanna was, I think, eighty three.

Four generations, not long before Nanna and Grandpa died. (Standing l to r me, Tanya, Tina, Grandpa. Seated l to r Mum, Nanna). Looks like Nanna's cancer was already advanced.

Grandpa died within three months of Nanna at eighty-nine. He'd been too upset to attend her funeral. He died when he was staying at my mum's bungalow in Leigh-on Sea where she lived with my stepfather Jim (it was actually his bungalow – Mum never on principle took a penny from the sale of the Recreation Avenue bungalow). Poor Grandpa had a stroke in his bedroom and fell against the door so it couldn't be opened.

William Richard Bell (Grandpa) was born on Midsummer's Day 1883 and was the man Olive married. He was tall and handsome and even in old age he walked with his back as straight as a die. This is my very first memory of him:-

Grandpa is standing in his calm, easy way at the bottom of the stairs. The hallway is light with sun coming through the glass panels of the front door. My big, black pram with its hood and huge wheels stands at the bottom of the stairs. The stair carpet is held in place by polished brass stays and the wood of the treads is exposed on either side.

I crawl towards the edge of the top stair. Grandpa tenses but before he can move I'm over the edge and tumbling, knocking, banging my way down. This is the very strangest set of sensations. It's loud and disorienting and relentless but doesn't last long and I don't feel any fear or pain.

Grandpa with his father in the wicker sidecar, mid-1920's.

As far as I know I didn't break any bones or suffer serious harm. Grandpa must have had some explaining to do … or perhaps I was as right as rain and he never mentioned it to my mum.

I have a small and very scratched sepia photograph (below) of my grandfather who fought at the battle of the Somme. In the photo he seems to be in military uniform resting on a camp bed reading what looks to be a magazine called *The Swan*.

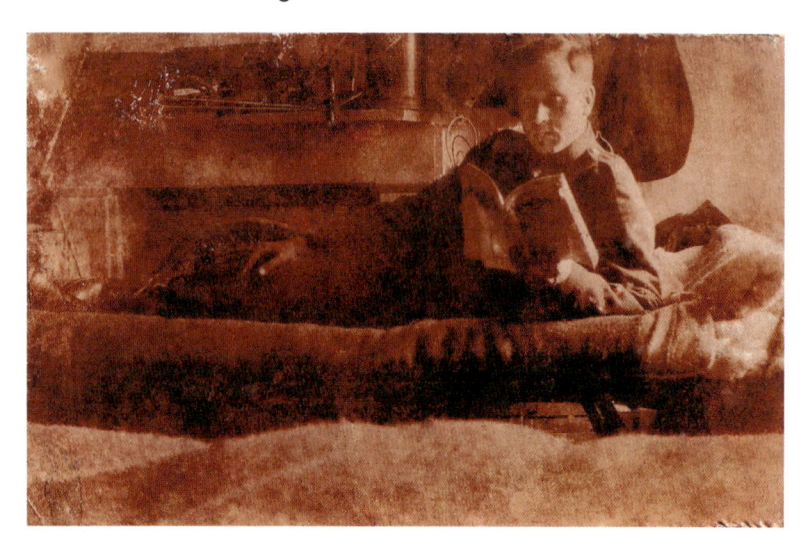

There's no indication where the photo was taken but as you can see there's a rather magnificent fireplace with a mantelpiece in the background. I suppose it could be some Officers' quarters in France or perhaps the photo was taken during Grandpa's training.

The British Expeditionary Force fought in France before the regular army arrived. They were volunteers, a bit like the Home Guard in the Second World War. It's quite possible that Grandpa was part of the BEF. Grandpa was thirty-one when WW1 broke out.

A while ago I met a man in a local supermarket selling poppies and dressed in First World War uniform. I got talking to him and every so often he asked me to hold his rifle so he had both hands free to sell poppies. I was amazed at how heavy it was. It was battered and scratched and had obviously seen a lot of service. I wondered how many Germans it had killed.

I can't imagine my gentle Grandpa walking over the dead bodies of his friends and colleagues.

Trees by WR Bell approx 1911.

The watercolour sketch book I have of his dates back to about three years before the outbreak of the war in 1914. 1911 seems to have been a very artistically productive year for him. That would have been round the time my grandparents married and many of the sketches are of the area near where Olive Fountain lived before she married. There's a sketch of the town of Honfleur in France. I know my grandparents went to France soon after they married and this sketch could have been done on that trip.

Barkingside by WR Bell 1911.

After the flurry of activity in 1911 in Grandpa's sketchbook there are no more sketches until 1933. I wonder if Grandpa was affected so badly by the war that he wasn't able to paint again for all that time. It seems quite possible.

Strange how early memories stand like bright little islands in a dark ocean of things forgotten.

Back to the cast of characters …..

Eileen Mary Bell – My mum. She wanted to be a nurse but her mum wasn't keen and instead she trained to be a shorthand typist and when she was about sixteen she joined the RAF as an Intelligence typist. During the war a German Doodlebug almost knocked her off her bike as she was cycling home from work. A few years ago I was visiting Verdun on a motorcycle trip and I insisted (in good humour of course) a young German apologise to me for Herr Hitler causing my mum distress. We shook hands and agreed to let the matter rest. I also insisted he apologise on behalf of the Luftwaffe for the bomb my fisherman friend Nigel dragged ashore in his net. We shook hands again and agreed to let that rest too.

Shorthand typing stood my mum in good stead but eventually, when she was in her forties, she got her wish and became an Auxiliary Nurse at Southend General Hospital. She loved it and kept her white uniform (albeit in places foxed brown with age) in her wardrobe until she died at eighty.

When she was in her forties my mum was prescribed Valium like many people (especially women) at the time – that would have been in the 1960's. Mum took the drug every day I think and became hopelessly addicted to it (like a lot of people at the time). Doctors used to hand out Valium and Librium at the time like sweets. Both are minor tranquilizers that help you sleep.

When Mum took herself off the Valium she suffered a complete mental breakdown. I remember her one day being extremely paranoid about a record I was playing in the living room while she was ironing. It was called *Rhythm and Blues All Stars* and she thought the lyrics were directed at her and got me to stop playing it.

These days doctors are more aware of the dangers of highly addictive drugs like Valium and are much more careful about prescribing them and giving repeat prescriptions – things were different in the nineteen-sixties.

Mum also kept her long-expired driving license because it represented another of her precious achievements – passing her driving test in, I think, her late fifties (round the early 1980's), having failed the first time in the 1950's.

Her parents, her children, her Jim, her few close friends, her nursing career, reading, her driving license and animals and birds – those were the big loves in my mum's life. As I write this on March 6th 2015 my mum's been dead eleven and a half years. Only now do the lovely memories of her bubble to the surface and the overriding tone of her life is that of kindness, gentleness and sensitivity. Mum, your spirit was (and is, I hope) colourful and beautiful. Your gentle soul touched so many lives and I miss you so much. God Bless (as your Jim would have said). The more the years pass the more I remember the good and worthwhile things about those who were (and are) close to me.

My first memory of my mum is this:-

It's a warm summer day. Mum is pegging white sheets on the line and I'm sitting on the grass watching her. The sky is unbroken blue and high above a thread of white vapour opens out behind a jet plane. In that instant my world seems a perfect place.

Cecil Howard Elford was my dad. He celebrated his birthday on June 10th and his headstone in Trefeglwys churchyard in mid-Wales proclaims him to have died at sixty in February 1977. He came from a poor family, left school at fourteen, apprenticed as a car mechanic and became a marine engineer and served on hospital ships during World War Two. He was a brilliant driver and would have loved to have been a racing driver. I'm sure he would have made it too, were it not a sport exclusively for sons of the rich. My dad was born with poverty all around him. He was never in debt as far as I'm aware and died with no money but happier than he had ever been (like my mum, he remarried). His second wife was a lovely Welsh lady called Elizabeth who had once been engaged but her fiancée was killed in World War Two. She had looked after her sick mother until she died, then her father until he died too. Dad and Elizabeth had only been married for a few years when Dad died. It was so sad that their married life was so short-lived (it may have been about six or seven years, I can't quite remember), and that Dad died a few years short of retirement age. Elizabeth went on to develop Alzeimer's disease and spent her last few years in a nursing home. Her twin brother Tom had taken his own life some years before. He'd been a sheep farmer all his working life and when he retired he passed on the farm to his son Christopher and his wife. I think suicide is quite common amongst farmers and I understand Tom (for no real reason) had been really worried about the farm.

Tom's daughter Maggie (or Margaret as I knew her) arranged the nursing home for her Auntie Elizabeth and also the sale of Elizabeth's house to pay the nursing home fees. Margaret was married with children and living in Nottingham and it wasn't easy for her to keep driving over to mid-Wales to see Elizabeth and sort things out for her (particularly as the Alzeimer's took hold of her mind). Maggie continued to visit Elizabeth in the nursing home right up to the end, even though Elizabeth had long been unable to recognize who her visitor was.

One of Dad's favourite books was *Speed* by Donald Campbell, the famous British land speed record holder. My dad lent me the book once. I remember it had a pale blue hardback cover and no dust jacket. It's still one of the most exciting books I've ever read.

The first I remember of my dad is standing with him by the side of a busy London street. I was born in St Alfege's Hospital, Greenwich in the autumn of 1951. The hospital is no longer there but the saint's name is preserved in names in the area. After that we moved to Croydon and the memory is most likely of one of those two places. It's a grey, drizzly day and we're waiting for something exciting to happen. After a while old cars approach us and drive past. That's all I can remember but it must have been on the route of the London to Brighton old crocks rally. What I remember most of all is my dad's excited anticipation of the cars arriving and how close I felt to him as he held my hand.

MY DAD'S LOT

Grandfather Elford – My dad's father, except he's unlikely to have been called Elford. There's no reliable information about this guy, only a rumour. The man who fathered my dad's brothers and sisters (who by rights should have been the real Grandfather Elford) was killed round about 1916 in some sort of accident, a year or two before my father was born, so my dad's father was some other man. Elford is my real surname. Cora Jane (my dad's mum) and her friend Mrs Frost used to travel the ten miles or so from Crediton to Exeter on the bus once a week to visit Mrs Frost's brother, an antique dealer. It's rumoured that he was my paternal grandfather, but Cora Jane took the secret with her to the grave so it may or may not be true. My sister says it's possible that Cora Jane couldn't afford the registration fee and may have delayed entering my dad's details for a year or two. If that's the case then it's probable that the real Grandfather Elford was his dad ... but my dad was the only one to have curly hair and Mrs Frost's brother had curly hair! It's a mystery we'll never solve.

After the real Grandfather Elford died his wife was left with I think seven children and no income. She kept the five boys and gave away the two girls, Molly and Gwen, to Dr Barnado's. They were shipped off to Canada and each ended up living with different

This was when Dad went to Crediton in the early 1960's for a family reunion. (l to r) Dad, his mum Cora Jane, his brother Jack and his two sisters Molly and Gwen and their husbands.

Mum, Dad, Tina as a baby and Mum's parents in happy times.

Canadian families. Molly and Gwen married Canadian men and each had families.

I sometimes wonder if there was some sort of financial arrangement between Cora Jane and the Exeter antique dealer who in all likelihood was my dad's father.

Some time in the early 1960's my dad drove on his own to Crediton to take part in a family reunion. Molly and Gwen were there with their husbands as well as three or four of the brothers (brother Victor disgraced himself by thieving and spending time in prison. He moved to Coventry to find work and I doubt if he was welcome at the reunion). The others all got together and by all accounts had a great time. There was an article in the local Crediton paper about it with a photo of them all. I imagine Molly and Gwen had forgiven Cora Jane by then for giving them away (the reason she gave away the two girls was because the boys would have had greater earning potential).

Cora Jane Blackmore – My dad's mum. *Lorna Doon* was written by one of my ancestors, RD Blackmore. I'm rather proud of the fact that one of my lot wrote one of the most famous books in the world. Cora Jane's and RD's lives overlapped and my sister thinks that RD was Cora Jane's great-uncle – which would make him my great great great uncle.

Early family holidays were always spent in Devon, seeing many of my dad's relatives. All of us up at first light. Mum panicking a little but coping. Dad excited by the forthcoming holiday and in a really happy mood. He's serviced, cleaned and polished the Hillman Minx and all the luggage is packed in the little boot, the roof rack and crammed into any bit of space inside that isn't taken up by us. Mum, Dad, my sister Christine (who was born on Friday 13th June 1947) and I pack ourselves into the little black car with its leather upholstery and off we go on the big adventure. No motorways in those days – this was the late 1950's. I don't remember that car with its inefficient side valve engine ever breaking down but Dad was a brilliant mechanic and engineer and always carried a tool kit and would have had the knowledge and confidence to fix it himself by the roadside should anything go wrong.

He'd encourage that little car up the steeper hills when she was threatening to run out of puff before reaching the top. She always made it, sometimes in first gear, and in those days it was quite an art selecting first gear on the move with a gearbox that had no synchromesh on the lowest gear – you had to double declutch and get the revs just right or there was an embarrassing and loud crashing of gears.

We went from Southend in Essex to Crediton in Devon (about ten miles from Exeter). Crediton was my dad's birthplace and he had many relatives in the area. We headed first for his mum's little cottage in Howard's Place, Dean Street (My ancestor Howard Elford must have had great family significance because my dad and all his brothers had Howard as a middle name) and Devonshire Grandma (Cora Jane Elford) lived in a small court of cottages which also bore his name.

Looking at a map now, I think we would have taken the arterial road to London (it's thirty miles or so to the outskirts), then crossed the river and made our way south to eventually join the A30. Box Hill, Basingstoke and Stonehenge are pretty much the only places I can remember now. We used to picnic in a lovely wooded area near Box Hill in Surrey. The car would have a rest and Dad would get the little paraffin stove going to boil a kettle of water for tea. It was all so lovely and innocent somehow and Dad was always in a cheerful and mischievous mood at holiday times. He loved the adventure of getting us all safely to the heart of Devon.

The other stop I remember was at Stonehenge. In those days you could go right up to the stones and touch them. They seemed impossibly massive when you were standing beside them.

It was a long, long way and we'd arrive in the early evening. Dark rooms, Crediton Church (where my Dad had been a choirboy) and deep, dark Devonian voices are what I remember most about those holidays. Those voices sometimes sounded like they were speaking another language, so rich and strong was the dialect. Mum later told me she always felt uncomfortable with Cora Jane and Dad's brothers and their wives. She was from a middle class and well-healed family; they were country folk who thought she was a bit posh. The two extended families were poles apart and had little regard for each other.

My dad was a very clever man. As well as being a brilliant engineer and car mechanic he was generally good with his hands and was always making things out in his garage. He made some excellent pieces of furniture of his own design such as a bedside cabinet he made for my sister. It was a very elegant and practical design. He was also capable of turning his hand to plumbing, electrical work and building. A very useful man to have around.

After Devonshire Grandma died in the early 1960's when I was ten or so we spent our family holidays in East Anglia. We'd rent a cliff top caravan for a week or maybe two, I can't remember now. Those were lovely holidays and I preferred them to the Devonshire ones.

My favourite holidays were spent in a caravan at Dunwich in Suffolk. I remember the caravan being not so far from the cliff edge and there being a rickety wooden staircase down to the beach. Early in the morning before most people were up you could look out of the caravan window and see scores of rabbits.

If the weather was bad we'd go for a drive and visit interesting villages and ancient churches.

The cliffs of Dunwich were (and still are) being rapidly eroded and crumbling into the sea. Most of the original town is now submerged.

Dunwich was where my dad taught me to drive. I was probably ten or eleven years old. The caravan site was big and there was a lot of space between the caravans. My dad taught me the rudiments of driving a car and before long I was able to drive confidently around the caravan site. He told me not to tell Mum what we'd been up to (she would not have been happy!) and it felt good to share that secret with my dad.

One year my sister's boyfriend Roger visited our caravan site for a day on his 600cc Norton Dominator motorbike. This was a few years before Roger sold me his Norton. It had no kick start and I had to run down the road with it, leap on side saddle then let out the clutch in second gear in order to start it.

One time I was on the A12 on my way to visit my sister Tina and Roger near Colchester (by that time they'd married) and the bike suddenly slowed down and came to a very rapid halt. I left it by the roadside and hitch-hiked home. A day or two later my dad took me up there with a trailer on his car to collect it. It was still there, untouched, by the roadside. Back home I helped him strip down the engine to try and find the cause of it seizing and sure enough we found a blocked oilway to one of the two cylinders. The seizure had been so sudden that it bent the con rod quite dramatically. We replaced what was necessary and after that the bike ran perfectly.

My Norton wasn't happy doing just thirty in top gear and I collected three speeding tickets which resulted in a year's ban from driving. When that happened I sold the bike and set off travelling round Europe for a couple of months with my friend Paul.

One year on our way to a caravan holiday my sister Tina had a transistor radio playing in the back of the car (transistor radios were pretty new then). *"I Get Around"* by the Beach Boys came on and I loved that song straight away and still do.

My mum used to say the only time Dad was happy was when he was on holiday and there may have been some truth in that.

Our last family holiday was probably when I was about fourteen. After that relations between my parents deteriorated into a full scale war and my mum walked out for the last time when I was about seventeen I think.

Before their marriage started breaking down my mum and dad often went to the Westleigh Baptist Church on a Sunday morning or evening and I went to the Sunday school in the afternoon. My teacher was a lovely gentle soul called Mr Dawes who used to turn up just before Christmas with a present of a model aircraft kit.

A new church was built in the early sixties and I'm not quite sure how I got involved but I read the very first lesson in the new church.

I remember the Reverend Bolton coming round one day and I stood on a chair in the living room and read him the lesson. He was obviously impressed because I got the job!

Strangely, I wasn't at all nervous. I went up to the lectern in the pulpit and did my stuff. They said my voice was as loud and clear as a bell.

*   *   *

I was extremely shy as a boy and teenager and could never bring myself to look anyone in the eye when I was talking to them.

I'm not so shy these days and make a point of looking people in the eye when they're talking to me. Like a lot of people I let my eyes wander when I'm addressing someone. I can't concentrate on what I'm saying properly if I look people in the eye when I'm doing the talking. I find it a real distraction.

My dad was also a very shy man. When he had a little house in Wales after the split from my mum I remember seeing a book on a bookshelf called *How to Overcome Shyness*. He never went to pubs or socialized much. I think he was happy with his family group or maybe just one or two friends.

I always felt out of place with a large group of people and something like a discotheque I found positively paralysing.

*   *   *

The winter of 1963 was a bad one. It snowed and snowed and remained very cold so the snow turned to thick ice on all the pavements and was treacherous for many weeks.

I think it was that year that a back boiler exploded in a house in Cricketfield Grove, Leigh. They used to install thick iron back boilers behind open fires and the fire would heat the water. A clever idea but could be extremely dangerous if the pipes froze and the water couldn't circulate. The water would turn to steam and create huge pressure inside the boiler which would ultimately explode and blast the burning fireplace into the living room.

It was after a family wedding and the wedding guests were at the house with the fire alight. A huge explosion blasted a massive hole in the outside wall and killed the married couple who lived there. Their daughter was severely disabled by the explosion and her boyfriend was also injured. Strangely enough I now live next door to the son of the deceased couple's daughter. His grandparents died before he was born. Other people may have been injured too, I don't know.

I remember my dad taking me round there (it was only a couple of streets away) to show me the big hole in the fireplace wall. He then showed me the pipes in our loft and impressed on me how important it was to make sure they were properly lagged to prevent them freezing up.

You'd get no warning with a back boiler blowing up, just a huge explosion from nowhere.

*   *   *

I'm in the sidecar of my dad's motorbike. I must be about three or four. It's a big, noisy bike. My dad wears a heavy coat and leather gauntlets.

All my life I've loved motorbikes.

When I was about fifteen I was given a sad-looking Mobylette moped. I stripped it down completely, including the engine (with the help of my dad's guidance), painted it brown and cream, renovated the little engine and put it all back together. It looked great and rode like a dream. I rode it (completely illegally) round all the local streets, up and down the Prittle Brook path and round and round the apple tree in our garden.

After I'd had a lot of fun out of it I sold it to my friend Andy's sister.

My first proper bike was a Norton 250 Jubilee. That would have been when I was sixteen. It was a fantastic bike to learn on. Two cylinders and it looked and felt a whole lot bigger than 250cc. It was silver in colour with lots of chrome and didn't have the big cowl over the rear wheel like the early ones did. It was named the Jubilee to commemorate Norton's diamond jubilee (they began in 1898). They made the bike from 1958 to 1966. It had the smallest engine ever made by Norton and was the first Norton to have a unit construction engine and gearbox (i.e. both in the same casing).

It was a lovely bike and I rode it around for a year or so, passed my test on it then sold it on.

After the Norton Jubilee I inherited Roger's Norton Dominator, I think it had been built in 1956 (I think the first year of their manufacture).

Tina and Roger were forever going up to the 59 Club in East London with their mates in their leather jackets and ice blue jeans. They were Rockers. Real ton-up kids, often exceeding 100 mph on the A127. This was before there was a 70 speed limit. In those days you could go as fast as you liked and be within the law as long as you rode safely.

The 59 Club originated as a youth club in 1959 in Hackney and in 1962 Father Bill (Bill Shergold) visited the then notorious Ace Café on his own motorcycle and met up with the 'Ton Up Kids' and then held a service and blessing of bikes at his church.

After that the 59 Club (which was a registered church charity) attracted thousands of young motorcyclists who joined and turned it into a motor cycle club where they could go to meet other Rockers, listen to rock 'n' roll on the juke box and drink coffee.

More than fifty years later the club is still going strong and has members all over the world.

After I'd passed my test it just so happened that Roger wanted to sell his bike because he was getting married to my sister and he gave me first refusal. I jumped at the chance to own his bike and bought it from him. By then he'd customised it by fitting clip-on handlebars directly onto the fork legs, a single seat, a five gallon petrol tank, swept-back exhausts, an oil tank that had been raced round the Isle of Man and various other bits and pieces to make it into a café racer.

I couldn't believe my luck .

When I got the bike I stripped it right down (this time without the help of my dad), hung the Featherbed frame up on wires in the garage and painted it a deep metallic green. The fibreglass tank was almost white and the bike looked brilliant when I reassembled it.

Roger had removed the primary chain cover to make the bike look more like a café racer and the dry clutch and primary chain were exposed and whizzing round only inches from my left foot. After I'd had the bike for a while I was prosecuted for that ("dangerous revolving parts") and at the same time received a speeding fine, a fine for no horn and points on my license. In the end, after three speeding tickets, I lost my license for a year but it just so happened that I was thinking of selling the bike anyway so I could go travelling round Europe with my friend Paul, so I wasn't that fazed by the ban.

*   *   *

My busman's career was over after a few months. I resigned from the job and the money I'd got for my Norton (£55) was enough for me to go travelling with Paul for a couple of months or so.

Paul and I packed our rucksacks and set off on our big adventure – a hitch-hiking trip round Europe. We had no idea where we'd go or end up – although we both fancied the idea of Greece. We were both nineteen at the time and full of a desire to see the world and clear all the school stuff from our heads.

I'd got a 'C' grade in the Geography 'A' Level so now I had Geography and Economics … a town planning HND was suggested but I didn't fancy that and the only other course open to me seemed to be an HND in Business Studies. Although my dad was off the scene I was still trying to please him and the Business Studies course at Stoke seemed suitable. Those invisible strings are hard to cut.

Paul's dad gave us a lift to Kent Elms Corner in Leigh on the A127, the main road into London (we're about forty miles from the centre of London) and off we went.

Near Canterbury we got a lift from a young Canadian woman in a camper van who was on her way to the Netherlands. We travelled with her on the ferry across the English Channel and the first night we reached Knokke in Belgium. She made us vacate the van for the night and said if we came back in the morning she'd take us to Amsterdam.

We duly set off in the dark (with not a torch between us) and eventually stumbled upon a barn with an open door. We went in and in the dark we laid out our sleeping bags on the floor.

Early the next morning we were awakened by a man arriving for work. In the light we could see that we were in some kind of agricultural workshop and sleeping almost under his bench.

He couldn't believe what he was seeing. We couldn't speak his language and he couldn't speak ours.

We made our excuses (which he couldn't understand) and returned to the camper van. The Canadian woman was almost ready to leave and off we went to Amsterdam.

We spent one day and one night (sleeping in a building site) in Amsterdam before we set off again.

We were soon in Germany and got lifts which took us through Düsseldorf and Köln.

At some point in Germany we met Fred and Henry, two Dutch guys. Fred was in his early twenties, tall and slim with wild curly hair and John Lennon glasses. Henry was I should think in his early thirties. He was tall, intense, bearded and loped along. He seemed to have little with him except some canvases which he carried under his arm. I imagine he had painting materials in his rucksack. They'd teamed up and were travelling together. Henry's aim was to hitch-hike to India. I'm not sure where Fred was heading. They were a delightful couple of guys and being Dutch spoke pretty perfect English.

They were very funny. Fred was studying philosophy at university and Henry told us he'd been studying psychology which he described as 'the science of what makes you have a tick'. He also referred to coconuts as coco's nuts.

We met up with them several times on our journey because we were all heading in roughly the same direction.

Paul and I hitch-hiked our way into Bavaria and came to rest for an afternoon and night at Rotenburg, a little place near Stuttgart.

We went in a pub and got drunk with nowhere to stay. A man helpfully said we could stay at his house which turned out to be a bungalow with very odd sleeping arrangements. There were empty tins of mushrooms all over the place. It seemed the only thing the guy eat. He offered us some cold tinned mushrooms which we accepted because we were hungry.

The only bedroom had a double bed and a single bed. Paul and I shared the double bed and the strange man slept in the single one.

During the night on several occasions the man got up and urinated out of the window.

In the morning we had our breakfast of cold mushrooms. He opened a big cupboard and it was full of unopened tins of mushrooms.

We set off again for Munich then crossed the border into Austria and stayed a while in Salzburg. I remember we spent one night sleeping on a ledge under one of the arches of a river bridge.

After Salzburg we cross the mountains then travel down into Ljubljana in Yugoslavia.

Through Zagreb then Split and Dubrovnik on the Adriatic coast.

It's all a whirl of strangers in cars and being deposited wherever they stop. We don't linger too much in any place. We want to get to the warmth of Greece.

The turquoise Adriatic, Skopje with its minarets broken by an earthquake a few years before, a monastery at Pec (pronounced Petch) high in the hills.

We finally make it to Greece.

Down to Athens, a quick look at the Acropolis then who should we meet at the ferry terminal but Fred and Henry.

We show them a brochure we picked up with a photo of a little place on the eastern tip of Crete called Väi. It looks like Paradise with its palm trees, wide sandy beaches and turquoise sea.

Henry is seduced by the photo into being sidetracked from the India route and before we know it Paul, Henry and myself are on the ferry to Crete. I can't remember what happened to Fred.

A few hours later we step off the ferry onto Cretan soil at Iráklion.

Immediately Henry decides he's not going to like Crete and goes back to Athens on the next ferry. That was the last we ever saw of him. I sometimes wonder if he ever got to India.

Paul and I make our way by bus to Väi.

The photo wasn't lying. It really is a Paradise of sorts.

It's become a bit of a laid back hippy place but the locals seem happy enough about that – it's all good money being spent.

It's wonderful to be at what seems to be the end of our journey and it's a great place to relax, eat good food and drink some beer.

There's a glut of huge, juicy tomatoes and the growers are happy to give us them for free.

Paul meets a Canadian nurse and decides to travel with her and her charms rather than me. Who can blame him for that? Well I can but I soon get over it.

After a week or two of rest and relaxation I get the ferry back to Athens and decide to make my way to Istanbul.

*   *   *

I'm standing on the outskirts of Athens hoping for a lift when a lorry pulls up and out gets a lovely girl of about twenty. We get talking and it turns out she also wants to go to Istanbul so we decide to hitch together – it's better for both of us. She gets a measure of protection and I get to be with a young girl who has to do no more than hold her thumb out and the traffic stops.

She tells me she has escaped from an arranged marriage in Lebanon (that bit was probably true) and her name is Mona Lisa (that bit possibly wasn't).

Whatever her real name she's olive-skinned, dark-haired and beautiful.

We get lifts very quickly and in a lorry that stops for us she insists I sit between her and the driver in case his hand is tempted to wander.

We get a lift in a fire engine. I think it's new and being delivered. He takes us quite some distance.

It's quite a few hundred miles from Athens to Istanbul and we do it comfortably in a day.

The fire engine driver insists on demonstrating the siren and lights for us which amuses us all no end.

We get to the centre of Istanbul and decide to find something to eat and drink.

We're in a tea house when Mona Lisa hears two men talking in Arabic which she can of course understand.

She goes over to chat to them and comes back to me and says that they've invited her and myself to go to their bar with them for free alcohol.

I'm not easy about the idea and should have trusted my instincts because later that evening we got into big trouble with the Arab men.

*   *   *

The Arabs' car winds away from downtown Istanbul up a long, steep hill.

The driver pulls in to an unlit café and bar and turns off the engine. We all get out and one of the men opens up the bar and switches on some exterior lights and brings out some beer. I drink a couple and notice that Mona Lisa is looking very edgy.

After half an hour or so we get up to leave but the two men come after us. One of them grabs Mona Lisa and the other one grabs me.

Now I've never been in a fight before but I punch and kick and hit until he lets me go. I give him a last kick when he's on the ground just to make sure.

Mona Lisa lashes out too and gives the other guy a massive kick in the groin. He keels over and drops to the ground in agony.

I grab Mona Lisa's hand and we run off down the road towards the lights of the city.

When we get to the city centre we find somewhere for a glass of tea and talk about our experience. We're both pretty shocked. We could easily have been murdered. We part company and Mona Lisa goes off to her pre-arranged hotel and I never see her again. It's like that with travelling on your own. You meet up with people, spend some time with them then part company. I love it. It makes those meetings with other travellers very precious. You're both in the same place at the same time for much the same reasons and that's why you often get on so well.

I stay on the first floor of a traveller's hotel on a busy road. I share a room with a Swedish guy called Lars who's got some dope and we get stoned most days. I notice when I'm high that the traffic sounds really weird – loud and as though it's just outside the window.

Lars leaves a book he's just read lying around and I take a look at it. It's a thick hardback by a guy called Bhagwan Shree Rajneesh. There's a picture of him on the cover. He's a very beautiful-looking Indian gentleman with a big white beard and a woollen hat. He couldn't look more like my idea of a religious guru.

The first page captivates me and I just can't stop myself reading on. The book is a written account of Rajneesh answering questions from his doting disciples at his ashram in Poona, India.

By the time Lars gets back from wherever he's been I've read a good fifty pages.

Lars is delighted and tells me that right now he's on his way to Poona to meet Bhagwan and his disciples and possibly to give up everything and spend the rest of his life there. A loud alarm bell rings in my head but I can see how he's become completely seduced by the man and his teachings. His words are so seductive and seem to draw on the truth of all religions.

I make a mental note to pay a visit to a centre in Suffolk called Medina which has been set up by some of his disciples. Lars tells me I'll be able to buy one or more of his many books there.

I visit the astonishing Blue Mosque and my new friend takes me to a nearby food market and helps me choose food to take back and eat at the hotel.

One night we visit the local brothel area, not to sample the goods but to experience the atmosphere.

The little houses where the prostitutes live with their families are arranged around a big, open, dimly-lit square with a few trees in the middle. They flaunt their wares in downstairs windows, much like they do in Amsterdam.

Everywhere are shadowy men in dark clothing checking out what's on offer. Every now and then a man disappears into one of the houses and a curtain is drawn across the window.

It's a fascinating place but I wouldn't want to spend too long there. It feels too dangerous and somehow strictly for the locals. Someone told me it's government regulated.

*　　　　　　　　　*　　　　　　　　　*

There's a little place called *The Pudding Shop* a little way from where I'm staying. If you're travelling through Istanbul on the way to India or going the other way you're bound to end up at *The Pudding Shop*. It's like the meeting of the small ends of two funnels – the big end of one being India and the other being London.

I often eat and spend time in *The Pudding Shop*. The food is cheap and the company generally interesting and good.

I'm running out of money – I've only enough for a few more days.

Someone tells me that I could sell my Levi jacket in the bazaar for a lot of money. Levi jackets and jeans are hard to get hold of here and command a very good price.

I take a walk through the bazaar and approach several clothing shops. They all offer more or less the same amount for my jacket so I sell it to the highest bidder.

I make enough money to survive another couple of weeks but I'm getting tired of travelling and want to get home as quickly as possible.

I see a note in *The Pudding Shop* from someone who is travelling back to London and wants another person to share the cost of the trip. I become the third person in the Land Rover and I have more than enough money to contribute to the diesel and buy food on the way home.

The journey is uneventful and takes us, I think, about three days. We drop the other guy off in Paris and then head for London.

The most memorable thing about the trip was our detour to Dachau concentration camp, which is now a museum. It's the most harrowing place I've ever been and is pretty much as it was when it was operational. I remember most the striped uniforms that the inmates had to wear, the gas chambers and the beautiful white sculpture done after the war by an Israeli which is very long and suggests entwined human forms.

*   *   *

It's August 1970 and three of us are in an old Morris Oxford on our way to the Isle of Wight festival. All spare space is taken up by our camping gear. I've borrowed my sister's sleeping bag and bought a cheap tent and a little stove and kettle.

Last year Dylan was the top act. This year it's Hendrix. There are thousands of people making their way along the road as we crawl towards the festival site. They wear hats and flowers and colourful clothing and carry bags and tents and are generally happy and carefree. It must be like a mediaeval pageant.

Me and Tanya not long after the Isle of Wight Festival 1970

I've brought enough dope with me to last the six days as long as I don't cane it too much.

We get to a massive camp site and set up our tents.

When I've set up my tent I have a celebratory joint and cup of tea while I sit inside and watch the circus of people passing.

It's a truly amazing feeling being part of such a huge festival. The rumour is that there will be even more people than there were at the Woodstock festival which only finished a few days ago. The crowd there was half a million strong.

I don't really see much of my friends after that. We kind of go our separate ways, enjoying the atmosphere, the food stalls, the performers moving among the crowd and of course the music. Occasionally we come together to talk about what we've seen and done.

The line-up is fantastic.

Jimi Hendrix, Miles Davis, Jethro Tull, Ten years After, Chicago, The Doors, The Who, Emerson Lake and Palmer, Joni Mitchell, Joan Baez, The Moody Blues, Leonard Cohen, Donovan, John Sebastian and Taste to name a few!

In all there are about fifty main stage acts and other bands are playing outside the main arena.

By the time we get to the last night I'm so tired and stoned that I fall asleep not far back from the stage and entirely miss Hendrix's performance when he comes on in the early hours of the morning.

It turns out it's his last major gig because a few weeks later he's dead.

If I'd have known he was going to die (at twenty-seven in London) I'd have made more of an effort to stay awake! There's a line from a song that goes something like *"I turned around and you were gone."* I guess life's like that. Some babies only make it into this world for a few minutes and some people live till they're a hundred and ten. It takes no time at all for a heart to stop beating.

*   *   *

I'm at college sitting in a toilet cubicle. I had to get away from the economics lecture. I had to be on my own so I came here. I'm not doing anything, just sitting.

Today started ok but during the morning a terrible, terrible darkness descended into me. It's got hold of my soul and it's wringing it so hard.

I know what it is. It's depression. If this is what my life's going to be like from now on then I don't want to be alive.

I'm walking back to the flat with my head and soul full of darkness.

I reach the flat and get into bed with my clothes on. This feeling has hijacked the centre of me. I lie still with my eyes closed. The awful heavy blackness wells up into my head like black treacle and paralyses my spirit.

*   *   *

When I was at college in Stoke-on-Trent one weekend (when I was feeling well) I visited my sister and her then husband Roger. At the time they were living in a rented flat in Shrewsbury. I think I was babysitting their baby daughter Tanya.

Tina and Roger went out for the evening and I decided to do a picture of the Blue Mosque in Istanbul which I had visited a while earlier. I made a black ink pen drawing of the mosque then used blue watercolour for a wash. The effect was really beautiful. I remember taping that drawing to a wall in the college flat in Northwood Court in Stoke, but I don't know what happened to it. I wish I still had it.

*   *   *

Is that the stars in the sky or is it the rain falling down?

I'm listening to some Hendrix in the living room of the college flat. The other guys are out so I'm on my own and it's a Saturday afternoon. The sun's high in the sky.

Ohh, there ain't no light nowhere.

I'm feeling great. I went out and bought a little watercolour set, a few brushes and a small pad this morning.

I'm sitting at the table where I can see over Hanley to Burslem in the distance.

I've filled a couple of old jam jars with water and I'm trying to paint the way I feel. The colours spread and flow rich and bright.

Colour volcano

Cadmium yellow pale and dark, scarlet, alizarin crimson, cerulean blue and ultramarine. Even the names are evocative of beautiful things.

The colours melt and bleed into each other and form other colours.

I love this.

The resulting little picture is like a volcano having erupted colour.

Manic-depression is touching my soul.

Feeling sweet feeling
Drops from my fingers

Jimi Hendrix sings.

I'm in good company.

       *   *   *

I'm so unwell during the second year of the Business Studies course that I take to my bed for days at a time. The others go off to college and leave me to it.

Now and then I walk to the nearby supermarket to buy food. I don't bathe and my hair and beard are very long. I must look like a tramp but I haven't got the energy to do anything about it.

One weekend my dad is staying at my sister's place in Shrewsbury and I arrange to go over there for Sunday lunch.

When I get there I relax into a strange state of mind. I let it take me over. I haven't got much choice.

I sit on the side of the bath in a kind of daze and eventually my sister comes upstairs to see where I've got to.

I've slipped away into a peculiar world. It's not a world of depression but somewhere where everything seems disjointed and not at all right.

My sister says I'd better stay the night and not drive back to Stoke.

I share a room with my dad.

That night I wake up and there's a horse's head as plain as day shining out of the dark and it's talking to my sleeping dad. It's a very gentle horse. Not at all scary, just very odd and rather funny.

Maybe this is the LSD having its effect some months after I took it.

I know now that I was suffering from what used to be called manic-depressive psychosis (I guess these days it's called bipolar psychosis) and the manic-depression was probably triggered by taking LSD.

I'm philosophical about it these days. On the one hand I've suffered hugely over the years with the most terrible and disabling depression but on the other hand manic-depression has made me an artist. If I had to choose between a life where I was stable and my own roller coaster of a life, without a doubt I'd go for the latter.

I woke up one morning and the psychosis had gone and I felt absolutely fine and creative again.

I went back to Stoke a few days later.

*   *   *

I'm too unwell to sit the final exams and the college gives me a prediction of how well they thought I might have done. (They thought I would have passed).

I return to Southend and move in for a while with Mum and Jim.

In the local paper I see an advert for trainee computer programmers at Customs and Excise in Southend. I apply for a job and attend a day-long interview and suitability tests.

I don't do well enough for computer programming but they offer me a job as a computer operator, which I accept.

It's early 1973.

* * *

Tanya, Mum and my stepfather Jim Burden.

One of the earliest business computers was made by English Electric and was called the LEO, which stood for Lyons Electronic

Organiser, It had been developed in the 1950's to work on Lyons payroll.

When I arrived at Customs in 1973 they were still using a LEO computer to work out the monthly UK trade figures. The machine was being run down to make way for an ICL System 4 machine, a more modern and much faster computer.

The LEO had hundreds of valves and every day engineers had to replace any burnt out ones.

I never learned how to operate the LEO myself and went straight on to the ICL machine.

The machine itself filled a big computer hall and had I think twenty tape decks which were processing information twenty-four hours a day, seven days a week.

In the middle of the hall was the operator's console and from there you controlled the operation of the machine.

I have some very happy memories of working at Customs. I made some good friends (two of whom, Martin and John, I still see regularly. A third, Ian, who was my shift leader has become extremely reclusive and I hardly ever see him these days.)

Ian Glascodine going for the big shot.

Martin Hart and Eric the Cat taking a bit of time out

The computer operations division, being such a specialised department, was a law unto itself with very little outside interference.

Two hour lunch breaks were the norm and the Victoria Station buffet bar just over the road was a favourite place to go and sometimes get fairly drunk before returning to go online and deal with the big computer.

A short time after I started at Customs I found a flat in York Road, Southend and moved out of Mum and Jim's place. It was too expensive for just me so I advertised in the *Evening Echo* for two flat mates. Two Irish guys responded, Kieran, a Protestant from the North and Flannan, a Catholic from Limerick. They both worked for the *Beneficial Finance Company* and agreed to set aside their religious differences for the sake of a quiet life and we lived there until I found a better flat in Woodfield Road, Leigh-on-Sea and the three of us moved in there. Kieran went on to become a manager in the same organisation and Flannan went on to become a London bus driver which was much more to his liking. Flannan was one of the most funny and delightful people I've ever known.

The flat had three bedrooms and over the next few years quite a number of people came and went.

Upstairs lived a weird couple called Mr and Mrs Scarr. He was a fat osteopath with a lascivious leer and she was aloof, buxom and strange with long dark hair down to her ankles which she always kept in a tight bun. I only saw her unfettered hair once.

Martin Hart was also there in the early days. He also worked as a Customs computer operator. I still see Martin regularly all these years later. He has a fantastic sense of humour and feeling for the bizarre.

Before Martin moved in to the Woodfield Road flat he shared a house with Pete Smalley and one-eyed Ron in South Benfleet. One day Martin arrived at work with a box full of kittens. He opened the box and soon the little creatures were running about creating havoc all over the place. They were running about in the offline area, the online area (where the big computer was) and one or two even got under the floor. It was all very funny but I'm not sure if he found homes for any of them, which was why he brought them in.

Someone else I still see from those computer days is John Hazard. John now lives with his wife Paula in Fulking, West Sussex in the rather splendid Laurel House.

John Hazard on my balcony. Southend Pier is in the background (the longest pleasure pier in the world).

One lunchtime John and I decided to visit a local car breaker's yard in his red MG 1300 to look for a part for my car. It had been very rainy and the breaker's yard was thick with mud. I got my trousers and shoes in a dreadful state and John insisted I take them off before getting in his car. He drove to the Woodfield Road flat and I got out trouserless and went into the flat for some clean trousers and shoes before going back to work.

One morning I got up and went to the vestibule inside the main front door to see if I had any mail. The flat door closed behind me. The trouble was I was naked with no way of getting back in. I did the only thing I could do and rang the bell to the upstairs flat. When Mr Scarr (I was glad it wasn't his wife) opened the door I was standing there with a hand over my naughty bits. I explained the situation to Mr Scarr and asked if I could borrow something to wear so I could go round the back of the building and let myself in the back door.

He returned with a translucent plastic mac which was better than nothing and I went round the back in it and let myself in.

The neighbours hated us. We were young, noisy and had frequent riotous parties.

Round the time Flannan and Kieran left the flat my sister left her husband Roger (he of the Norton motorcycle) and came back to Southend with her little daughter Tanya with nowhere to live so I offered them a home in the flat where they stayed for the next few years.

Tina's husband didn't forgive her for taking away his little girl and refused to pay any maintenance unless the bailiffs turned up to take away his expensive car. It didn't just hurt Tina of course, it hurt Tanya as well.

Being the sort of person she is she didn't let it get her down and did whatever was necessary to support her child. I think Tanya was about three when they moved in.

Tina worked as a barmaid at the *Railway Hotel* in Southend, always a good music pub. I've played there myself with my occasional band *The Rocket Blues Band*.

THE ROCKET BLUES BAND

THE RAILWAY HOTEL
TUES 13TH OCTOBER
9PM FREE ADMISSION

Tina also had vast quantities of soft toys delivered which she stuffed and stitched. The living room was overrun with them but it was delightful and Tanya loved them.

Like me, Tina had always been very artistic (it's in our blood, like travelling) and eventually did a ceramics course at the Southend College of Art and Design (as it then was) which she loved. She went on to become a studio potter and made all kinds of beautiful

Tina stitching curtains at Woodfield Road.

things. I still have some bowls, a teapot and a casserole dish she gave me.

It was lovely having Tanya living with us. She was a delightful child.

Tanya at Woodfield Road

Each year for a few years I took Tanya on an adventure. One year we went to see the crown jewels, another year we went to the wonderful house at Syon Park just west of London. That was fantastic with huge tropical butterflies flying around and settling on us. Another year I took her to Winnie the Pooh country in Sussex and Norman Shelley read to us from Poohsticks Bridge. (Norman Shelley famously at the time used to read Winnie the Pooh stories on the radio).

A boyfriend of Tina's at the time was called Keith and he was a commercial artist. He was a rather dark character but painted a wonderful and colourful mural on old sheets of computer stationery which I got from Customs. It showed a band playing and completely covered one wall.

I was really into photography at the Woodfield Road flat (I still am) and converted the shed at the bottom of the garden into a darkroom. I used black plastic rubbish sacks to cover the windows and, much to the Scarr's irritation, ran an electric cable down the garden. I also had a hosepipe running to the shed because developing and printing your own films needs a lot of water.

Another of my sister's boyfriends was Simon Hill who lived in South Benfleet and was a frequent visitor to the flat. They went on to be together for several years.

Simon Hill and I off to a Roman party.

79

Simon retired at forty-five and has spent much of the last twenty years going on cycling adventures in the Far East, Australia and New Zealand. He reckons he's clocked up about fifty thousand miles which is the equivalent of cycling twice round the world!

When I was at the Woodfield Road flat I got the only pet I have ever owned – a little black and white cat I called Eric.

Eric the Cat

Martin bought a gerbil he called JJ after JJ Cale and kept it in a cage in his bedroom. One day when we were all out at work Eric pushed his paw through JJ's cage and extracted it through the bars, leaving a sort of gerbil-shaped hole in the cage. When Martin got home from work Tanya (who was four years old at the time) informed Martin that JJ wasn't well. Martin went in his bedroom and discovered a very dead JJ lying on the floor. I think Eric was magnificently clever to work out how to extract JJ from his cage.

I remember one of our parties had the theme of black and white. As usual the neighbors called the police. Someone was dressed as a policeman and they went and answered the door, much to the amusement of the real police.

The Scarrs truly hated us and were always complaining about everything.

In the end they bought the two flats. Mr Scarr started demanding inspections of the premises and took to wearing a strange kind of uniform – a double-breasted blazer and a kind of yachting cap. He must have thought it suitable Landlord clothing.

Next door was an old married couple who were up and down to the Catholic church it seemed several times a day. Pity they weren't a bit more godly in their behaviour.

They didn't like the sound of birds in the garden and would come out to scare them off by ringing a large hand bell.

They too complained even when there was nothing to complain about.

I went through a phase of putting large hand-written biblical quotations in the living room bay window aimed at them. Passing commuters on their way to Chalkwell Station were much amused.

I chose things like "Love thy neighbor" and the one about the mote in you brother's eye and the plank in your own.

*   *   *

The spells of depression came and went but somehow weren't as disabling as before. I never had any time off work because of depression that I can remember.

My creative highs were still very much there and as an antidote to the Civil Service I did a year's evening class in sculpture at Southend College which had been excellent for art since the early 1900's (and still is).

I absolutely loved the sculpture course. Our teacher was a lovely man called Bill Freeth and I immediately felt at home at the art college.

One of the young female Foundation Year students posed naked for us and I created a figure sculpture and cast it in resin mixed with powdered black soapstone. Some years later I had an exhibition at Southend Library and it was the only thing I sold apart from a watercolour self portrait which was bought by my friend John.

Evening Echo picture of me and the sculpture I did at the college.

I spent just over four years working for Customs in Southend then decided I wanted a change. I applied to move to the Bristol Collection (Customs divides up the country into what it calls Collections) as a Collection Officer. Now the stupid thing was that I had no relevant experience to do the job but because my seniority number was higher than anyone else's who applied I got the job. I never even had an interview. I understand that that ridiculous system doesn't exist any more.

I had friends in Bath. That's why I wanted to move down that way. My friend Paul (the guy I travelled round Europe with) was working as a dentist in Bath and sharing a flat with two other guys I knew from Paul's university days at Bristol.

I packed my Morris Oxford with stuff and off I went to start a new life in the West Country.

For a few weeks I slept on a makeshift bed in the living room of their flat then I found a room in a shared house in The Avenue, Bristol.

For me the Collection Officer job was a nightmare from day one.

As a Collection Officer you were posted to any part of the Collection to help out if they were a man or woman short. All the other Collection Officers had experience of working in the outfield – the work might include working at ports and airports, bonded warehouses, container depots and suchlike; anywhere a Customs presence was required. The only experience I had was with a big main frame computer which was of no use at all.

My first posting was to a bonded warehouse in Bristol where someone had retired or died. They really needed someone competent who could fit in straight away and help them out. They didn't have the time or the inclination to train someone up for the job.

My very first day there I felt alienated and disliked because I wasn't capable of doing the job. After a couple of days of hanging round in the office not knowing what the hell was going on they sent me up to the eighth floor which was full of wooden barrels of rum waiting to be bottled. The smell from the evaporating spirit was heady and glorious. They'd given me a little brass kit in a wooden box to check the specific gravity of some of the barrels. I also had to check the ullage (the amount of liquid remaining in the barrel after evaporation). Someone had reluctantly shown me how to check the ullage (with an ullage stick) and check the specific gravity and I spent day after day up there feeling slightly inebriated from the fumes and writing figures on bits of paper.

No one ever came to see me or seemed interested in the figures I was recording.

I was next sent to Avonmouth docks to an office where they dealt with ships' manifests and desperately needed a competent person to help them out. They quickly realised I was worse than useless and after a few days I was sent to a big container depot where the Officer had retired, leaving his assistant in charge. Again they needed a competent individual who understood the workings of a busy container depot. Then I turned up, knowing nothing about anything.

I was the only Officer there. Just me and my assistant.

Each day there was a constant stream of workers coming into the office brandishing bits of paper which needed stamping. In the end I just stamped anything that was put in front of me. I didn't give a toss. It wasn't my fault I didn't know how to do the job.

The depression was coming on strong again and I was finding it increasingly difficult to make it into work.

The creative mania was there too at times and one night I wrote a short story which I called *Life Goes On*. I sent it in to the BBC and it was accepted for broadcast on Radio 4.

One day I'd had enough of Customs and went into work and wrote out my letter of resignation. I addressed it to my boss in Bristol and put it in the out tray.

Not surprisingly no one tried to dissuade me from leaving. I worked out a bit of notice and then I was free.

I went back to Southend and moved in with Tina, Tanya, Martin, Simon and Eric the Cat who were all sharing Simon's house in Ramuz Drive, Westcliff.

I was so relieved to be free of the Civil Service. Because I'd been in their employ for less than five years, all the pension payments I'd made were returned to me rather than being frozen for retirement.

To help me get over the horrors of my time in the West Country I decided to go travelling for a while. I could think of no better way of spending my pension money than on an extended trip to Europe and maybe beyond.

*   *   *

I've just got off the Magic Bus from Victoria Coach Station to Athens. I'm shattered and dazed and didn't sleep at all for a couple of nights. The only time the bus stopped was to let us use a toilet or buy some supermarket food.

It was a cheap way of getting to Athens and I chatted to some interesting people on the bus but I wouldn't do it again. I'm going to need a few days to recover.

I fancy a trip to Egypt and I'm going to visit a couple of travel agents once I've found somewhere to stay and had some sleep.

* * *

I'm on a small *Olympic Airways* propeller plane on my way to Cairo. We're flying low over the Greek islands. The colour of the sea is a beautiful turquoise and the islands look enchanting from up here.

I've met a couple of guys on the plane and we've decided to make for the *Golden Hotel* which by all accounts is a fantastic traveller's hotel in Talaat Harb, one of the main streets in Cairo.

One of the guys is called Rory and he's from New Zealand. The other one is an American called Glenn. We're all about the same age and got on well straight away.

We check in to the *Golden Hotel* with Mr Farris who owns and runs it. He's a lovely old man of about eighty and is very cultured and knowledgeable about Cairo. He studied at Cambridge University.

I share a room with Rory to halve the cost.

Rory, Glenn and I decide to check out the Pyramids. Mr Farris suggests catching a bus to Giza. It's only a short journey from the centre of Cairo. The bus journey itself is an adventure.

We decide to climb up one corner of the Great Pyramid even though tourist police shout at us that it's forbidden, but we ignore them and in any case we can see people already on their way up.

The blocks at the base are huge and quite difficult to climb. As you get higher the size of the blocks decreases until near the top they're quite small.

On top of the Great Pyramid. l to r Rory, me, Glenn. Looking towards Libya.

The apex isn't a point but a pavement maybe five or six metres along each side.

The view from the top is of course magnificent. Stretching away to the west towards Libya is sand desert. To the east is the huge metropolis of Cairo.

On top of Great Pyramid looking towards Cairo.

View from the top of the Great Pyramid.

We smoke a cigarette as a reward for the climb (it took me about forty minutes), take some photos then head back down. We reach ground level in a few minutes. The tourist police have lost interest in us.

The Sphinx is every bit as beautiful and mysterious as people say.

We find a nearby tea house and order small glasses of sweet tea. Men are smoking sheesha pipes and the whole atmosphere is exciting and alien to our culture.

As we're drinking our tea a young boy of maybe nine or ten comes in to get some hot coals to take away. As he passes our table he invites us to his house.

In the big main room a hugely fat woman sits on the floor propped against a central pillar. She has an air of dominance and authority and members of her extended family are sitting around the room.

One of the men passes me a sheesha pipe which has cannabis burning in it. I inhale the neat fumes and quickly become very stoned. The other two guys do the same and before long we're all really getting into this wonderful experience in a big way.

The family feeds us and one of the guys tells us that it's a really special day – it's the day of the baby's circumcision party. He tells us we'd be very welcome at the party. We of course agree to go.

We're in the house for some hours and during the late afternoon the kid who collected the burning coals tells us he's ready to lead us to the party. He tells us not to speak to a soul on the way. We follow him through the back streets of Giza and arrive at a cul-de-sac with a stage erected at the end. Hundreds of people are sitting and waiting for the entertainment to begin.

The kid takes us to the front, just in front of the stage and an elderly male attendant with a big stick wades into the pool of children sitting on the ground. They flee in all directions and leave a space for us to get through.

We are clearly the guests of honour.

The same man turfs out three people sitting side by side in the middle of the front row so we can have the best seats in the house.

The entertainment begins with two little girls reading Arabic poetry.

When they've finished, to show their appreciation audience members pass notes of money towards the stage and the little girls collect it.

Act after act comes on, jugglers, singers, all kinds of entertainers. Each time people passing money towards the stage. The three of us are loving it and we're still really stoned.

The show goes on until well after it's dark.

When we leave, the same boy leads us through the streets to where we can get a cab back to the hotel.

*   *   *

As the days pass a rhythm develops. I spend a day or two out in the wonderful craziness of Cairo then need a quiet day staying in the hotel to recover.

One day I visit the Museum of Antiquities and see the astonishing contents of Tutankamen's tomb. His golden death mask is one of the most beautiful objects I have ever seen.

Other days I just walk around the old part of Cairo, visiting souks and absorbing the biblical atmosphere. Women dressed from head to toe in black glide past, the traffic is noisy and the air is full of wonderful smells.

A week or so into my stay at the *Golden Hotel* Rory decides to move on to another part of Egypt and I'm left with the room to myself. I ask Mr Farris if he has another room I can share and he tells me not to worry because he'll find someone suitable to share my room and in the mean time I can continue to pay the half rate.

A few days later I get in from a walk and find someone else in the room. We get on straight away. Mr Farris has done well. My new room-mate is an American called Bob from Fort Worth, Texas. He's in his early thirties and served in the Viet Nam war.

One night he was in a bunker with several other soldiers and the Viet Cong lobbed a hand grenade into the bunker. Two of the other men were killed and Bob lost half of one of his feet. As a result he was pensioned out of the army and decided to travel the world.

He had a nice big chunk of Red Lebanese dope and had an interesting way of smoking it. He'd break off a little piece and stick a needle in it. He'd then light the bit of cannabis and collect the smoke in an upturned glass. He'd tilt the glass a bit and inhale the fumes neat.

It was a method I'd never come across before and it got us stoned very quickly.

One day I suggested we get stoned then go in search of the step pyramid of Saqqara which I'd seen mentioned in a guide book. Bob was well up for the adventure and we set off mid-morning.

We took a bus first then got a lift on a donkey cart then walked the last part. We walked past water buffalo wallowing in irrigation ditches and at one point saw an old man using an ancient Archimedian screw to move water from one ditch to another.

Water buffalo wallowing in an irrigation ditch

We reached a village near the step pyramid (it may have been Saqqara itself) and were beset by hordes of children who were not used to travellers like ourselves arriving in their village. They grouped around us and helped us find the pyramid.

The Saqqara step pyramid is between the trees

We admired it for a while then made our way back to the hotel.

I met a lovely couple staying at the hotel. He was a New Zealander called Larry and she was a tall and elegant American called Martha. Their intention was to travel right down the east coast of Africa to the Cape then travel up the west coast until they reached North Africa. They reckoned on the trip taking about a year.

Martha had a bible with her and every day she read a few pages. Her intention was to read the whole book (old and new testaments) whilst on her travels.

One day they told me they were off to Alexandria for a week and why didn't I meet up with them there. They gave me the name of the hotel they'd be staying at and suggested I stay there too.

It takes a couple of hours on the bus from Cairo and the road is mostly flat and straight and cuts through sandy desert.

I find the hotel where Martha and Larry are staying and check in. Like a lot of Alexandria it has a French flavour about it.

I go out for a walk along the seafront and take some photos. There's a beautiful long white sculpture on the seafront and I walk around it taking photos.

Suddenly I'm descended upon by two army officers. First they demand I give them my camera but I won't give it to them and they demand the film instead. It seems I've unwittingly been taking photos of a military establishment. I open the back of my camera and give them the film. They say they will get it developed and return it to me if it's ok. I don't believe a word of it. Eventually they leave me alone and go away.

I go back to the hotel. An old French woman is taunting the hotel cat by seeing how far she can take it before the cat lashes out and scratches her. I'm pleased to see her get some nasty scratches on her hand.

One day Martha, Larry and myself go to the beach. We decide to go for a swim. Martha strips off to a bikini and we all wade into the sea and start swimming out.

A bunch of young men appears on the beach. There must be seven or eight of them. They all strip off to their pants and follow us into the water.

We decide later it was because of Martha in her bikini. Egyptian men rarely see exposed female flesh and seeing Martha must have excited them.

*   *   *

I'm on the train from Cairo to Luxor and I'm not feeling at all well. My stomach is churning and I've got a bad headache. I guess it's some sort of food poisoning. My carriage is almost empty and I'm able to lay out on the seat.

After many hours we reach Luxor and by that time I'm feeling a little better.

It's so hot here. Must be over forty degrees.

I find a hotel and decide to try and have an afternoon sleep. I'm on the first floor. I put my glasses on the sill by an open window.

When I wake up my glasses have gone. While I was asleep the window has swung shut and knocked my glasses outside. I look down from the window and see there's a skip directly underneath.

I go downstairs and explain to the manager what's happened. We go in the street and he grabs a passing boy and puts him in the skip to retrieve my glasses!

Luxor has the City of the Living and the City of the Dead. They are separated by the River Nile.

I discover it's so, so hot during the day that I need to do my business in the early morning and be back at the hotel by about eleven then stay there until it cools down in the late afternoon.

Early one morning I get the ferry over the Nile and on the other side (the City of the Dead) I hire a bicycle to cycle up to the tombs of the Pharaohs (the Valley of the Kings).

It's a wonderful experience standing in those tombs and being surrounded by ancient pictures and hieroglyphics, some looking as though they were painted yesterday.

The cycle ride back to the ferry is all downhill and I feel as though I'm being blasted by a hot air blower.

Another early morning I get the ferry to visit the Temple of Hatshepsut which is near the Valley of the Kings.

Three of us hire donkeys to take us up over the temple. Everything goes well until we're on the path over the temple and the three donkeys suddenly stop walking and refuse to go any further. The donkey keeper signals that he wants some more money. We give him some coins and as if by magic the donkeys start walking again!

     *   *   *

I'm about to board a small Russian cruise ship which is bound for Odessa. On the quay a big dog is sitting guarding a large rucksack. The owner of the rucksack turns up. He's a young German called Hans and his dog is called Bongo. It turns out I'm sharing a four berth cabin with them. Bongo occupies one of the lower bunks.

The voyage to Syria (which is where I'm getting off) takes a day or so and, because Egypt is such a poor country, the ticket was very cheap - fifteen Egyptian pounds which includes all meals (an Egyptian pound equates pretty much to an English pound).

The passengers are roughly half Russian and half Arab plus Hans, Bongo and myself. Meals are in two sittings – the first one is for anyone who isn't an Arab and the second is just for Arabs. Bongo eats in the cabin.

The Russian food is fantastic.

My ticket takes me as far as Latakia in Syria.

When I disembark I discover I should have acquired a visa and they hold me in detention until the visa is sorted and paid for. The visa is rather beautiful with its Syrian stamps and Arabic script. It's a transit visa and allows me to stay in Syria for one week.

Syrian visa

One place I really want to go to is Palmyra.

The bus journey takes several hours. At one point we pass through a bit of Lebanon for no more than a few minutes. Several children attach themselves to the outside of the bus and sell things like bags of sugar to the bus passengers inside. I guess these things must be cheaper in Lebanon than in Syria. As the bus approaches the border the children jump off.

I find a hotel in Palmyra and discover I'm sharing a four-bed room with two Syrian soldiers. We communicate as best we can but I don't speak Arabic and they don't speak English. Their rifles are propped up at the ends of their beds.

Syrian girls, Palmyra. In the background, a Roman fortress where I found a couple of Roman coins.

Palmyra smells strongly of sulphur. Someone tells me the sulphur springs rising from the desert are the reason the town is there at all.

I go for a walk to the Roman fortress nearby. As I'm approaching it two young girls in astonishingly brightly-coloured dresses come towards me. They let me take a photo of them. In the background is the Roman fortress on a hill. I climb up to the ruins and find two young Japanese guys also up there. As I'm looking round the ruins I find a couple of Roman coins lying on the earth. One of them bears the head of an emperor, the other one is too worn to make out what's on it.

*   *   *

I travel from Syria into Turkey and make for my friends' house in a town called Kayseri in the middle of the country. I stay with them for a week or so then travel by train to Istanbul where, once again, I sell my Levi jacket to get some money for the trip home.

I get good lifts from Istanbul and within a few days I'm home.

*   *   *

When I get back to Southend there's a letter from the BBC waiting for me with a transmission date for my short story. It's in a couple of weeks time.

I don't have any money or a job so I sign up with an employment agency and within a couple of days they send me to a plastics factory just off Progress Road, a local industrial estate.

They put me to work on an injection moulding machine which is being used to make a part for soda siphons. They impress on me the importance of making sure the previous part is properly ejected before pressing the button to inject more molten plastic.

All goes well until mid-afternoon when my attention wanders and I inject molten plastic into the mould before the previous part has been ejected. I call the foreman who curses me and says my mistake will cost the firm a lot of money – it'll take a maintenance engineer more than half an hour to clean up the mould.

They put me on something safe for the rest of the afternoon then tell me my presence is no longer required.

The agency then sends me to a factory called *No-Sag Springs* that manufactures car seats. About half the factory is taken up by huge six hundred ton presses which are used to press the rear seat pans from sheets of steel. The other half of the factory is given over to semi-automatic spot welding machines for making the front seat frames. An operator is required to turn the frame in between welds.

I get put on one of the big presses with a guy called Peter who's worked at the factory for years. We each take an end of a big steel sheet and feed it into the press. When it's in right I press a button. A guard rises into position and the top part of the press comes down to press out the shape of the car seat pan.

I was given a couple of pairs of leather-palmed gloves to protect my hands but after handling maybe twenty steel sheets the first pair is pretty much cut to bits.

Peter tells me that they never give you enough gloves because it costs them money. He tells me I'll need at least another five pairs to last until lunch time and if I see the foreman he'll reluctantly let me have them. He says that bad cuts and lost fingers are commonplace here. He then tells me a shocking story about a maintenance man in a similar factory. The presses have a standby mode when the motors are still running. A maintenance man had to repair a similar press to the one we're on. He forgot to shut it down properly and was inside the press between the two pressing surfaces and some kind of malfunction caused the press to engage and the surfaces came together and pressed the guy to a few millimetres thick. I imagine all the guy's blood would have squirted out.

The following day they put me on one of the spot welding machines. Within half an hour or so I've developed a rotten headache and feel quite sick. During the lunch break I see Peter and tell him I've got a bad headache. He tells me it's because the extractor fan above the machine isn't working and I'm breathing in some nasty fumes, including cyanide. He says whenever a factory inspector arrives for a planned inspection as if by magic all the extractor fans are working, then pretty much as soon as the inspector's gone some of the fans start to fail again.

I stick the job for a few weeks then ask the agency if they can find me something else. They send me to the Ford tractor plant in Basildon for an interview. They decide I'm suitable and I start the following Monday at seven-thirty. You have to clock in and out and if you're more than two minutes late you lose half an hour's pay.

*   *   *

My short story is broadcast on BBC Radio 4 and I discover what a lonely event it is having something you've written used on the radio. For some reason I couldn't listen to it as it was being broadcast (it was all a bit overwhelming) and listened to the recording I made later. It was called *Life Goes On* and was read by an actor called John Glover. The story concerned two interests of mine – motorcycling and life after death. A young motorcyclist has a race at an aerodrome with two other guys and ends up crashing his bike and becoming temporarily dead. While he's dead he has some strange supernatural experiences and is brought back to life by one of the other guys.

With radio work you get no feedback whatsoever. The programme goes out and is heard by hundreds of thousands of people then it's lost to the ether forever. A strange business.

My success with *Life Goes On* encouraged me to write more short stories, maybe half a dozen or so in total and all of which I sent to BBC radio but none of which was deemed suitable for broadcast. I'd struck lucky first time but found it impossible to duplicate my success.

One of my efforts was returned to me with a note from the Head of Radio Drama saying that my work showed definite potential and promise and would I like to go to Broadcasting House to discuss any other ideas I had with Alan Dury the Head of Radio Drama at the time.

I met Alan Dury and told him of a couple of ideas I had. He told me to go away and write them and submit them to him but I still couldn't repeat my earlier success and in the end I gave up submitting work to them. It would be some years before I submitted a half hour radio play to RTE Radio Drama in Dublin which was accepted for production and broadcast. They invited me over for the recording at their expense and I spent a great day meeting the producer, actors and sound technicians and sitting in on the recording of my play. More about that later.

*   *   *

At Ford's tractor plant they've put me on the final assembly line and I have to fit track rods. The partially-assembled tractor comes down the line towards you resembling an iron oxide coloured metal sausage hanging from the line by two massive chains. I'm provided with a big steel lever to move the front chain out of the way so I can fit the track rod properly. At first it's extremely difficult to keep up with the speed of the line but after a few days of it you become really fast and are able to work your way up the line and give yourself a cigarette break.

I spend a few months working at Ford's then a chance encounter with an old Customs computer colleague leads to me signing on with a computer agency where I can earn really good money.

The money's good but I quickly realise I despise the job (and some of the agency people I'm working with). It's clear to me that I was never much good at computer operating and I'm really not cut out for agency work.

Luckily an alternative avenue begins to open up. I've always been good at woodworking and I see a plan for a home-made woodturning lathe in a woodworking magazine. It seems simple enough – a washing machine motor, a couple of lengths of 4X2, a bicycle hub and various other bits and pieces. I get hold of everything required and build myself a woodturning lathe. It works pretty well and is solid enough for the wood not to chatter when turning.

I buy a few basic turning tools and Simon lets me take over the brick shed at the bottom of the garden which already has an electricity supply.

I teach myself the rudiments of woodturning from books and magazines and before long I'm making kitchen roll holders and dibbers for planting seeds and plants in the garden. My first efforts of course leave a lot to be desired but gradually the quality improves.

I really love turning. It's such a lovely process, making shavings peel off a spinning piece of wood.

I decide to look around for a second-hand lathe and see a Coronet Major with a saw bench and other attachments advertised in *Practical Woodworking* magazine. I contact the seller, who lives in Wallingford, Oxfordshire. The lathe comes with lots of tools and accessories and the price seems very reasonable. I agree to buy it and my friend Pete the boat builder who has a van says he'll take me down there to pick it up.

A few days later I'm the owner of a second-hand Coronet Major lathe and it's installed in the shed.

New ash handles for old tools – some of the first things I made on my new lathe. *(Photo by Annie Dearman)*

*   *   *

When we were at Ramuz Drive Martin started going out with a lovely lady called Vanessa. I got to know her brother Cliff quite well over the next few years. Cliff (who died a few years ago) was a sensitive and gentle man who loved music and played the guitar. I was very fond of him.

Martin Hart messing with his bike.

A friend of Simon's was Pete Taylor who at the time worked as a boat builder.

Pete built some fantastic boats during his boatbuilding career. He had to stop eventually because of back problems, but Pete, being the sort of guy he is, turned it to his advantage. He went on a *Microsoft* course and became a computer expert working for all sorts of companies including Prouts, a Canvey Island boat builders.

Pete Taylor on his narrow boat *The Imagine.*

At the time Pete lived at his dad's bungalow with his Scottish girlfriend Annie in Tyrell Road, South Benfleet.

We've remained the best of friends ever since. After Annie left Pete found a new woman (at a disco in Sussex, I believe). Her name was Pat and she had two daughters, Jo and Zöe. Pete and

Pat are still together (and married) and live these days in Devizes, Wiltshire.

Pat Taylor with her magnificent blue ball.

Pete and I went on a one day hang gliding course near Biggin Hill in Kent. There was a bit of classroom instruction then we were taken outside, given a hang glider and a radio helmet and told to run like crazy down a hill.

I took off all right but my radio helmet wasn't working and I couldn't hear the instructor frantically telling me where I was going wrong and what to do. I didn't realise it but I was heading for a disastrous crash into a hillside. The glider hit the side of the hill and I was catapulted forward and hit my head on the A-frame. Fortunately the helmet wasn't completely useless and saved me from any injury. I was pretty lucky to survive that crash unscathed, but it put me off hang gliding.

Pete did really well on the course and before long owned his own glider and flew it in various parts of the world. In the end he crashed it into the sea and wrecked it but bought another one to replace it.

I worked with Pete on quite a few occasions doing minor trim work on various boats and varnishing the interior of a lovely yacht which him and another guy were building in a transport yard on Canvey Island. We also worked together building a porch in Leigh and on repairs to an old house near Southminster.

I used to love working with Pete. He was super competent and super efficient and always did a fantastic job. Even their house in Devizes has a nautical feel about it because the furniture and cupboards he's made would look good on a boat.

*   *   *

I just can't bear this dreadful computer operating work for much longer. The depression is hitting me hard at times and I've had to take some time off work (although I didn't tell them the real reason – I just said I wasn't well).

When I'm at work all I can think about is getting back to my lathe and designing things to make.

I've managed to put aside a fair bit of money from the agency work and one day I decide I'm going to tell them that I only want to do another week at Southwark Council, which is where I've been working for the last couple of months or so, and then finish.

I can't wait for Friday to come around then I'll be free of computer halls hopefully for ever and a new chapter of my life will begin.

*   *   *

New stoppers for old bottles. *(Photo by Annie Dearman).*

I get hold of all the woodturning books I can find, and any ones I can't buy I borrow from Southend Library. I also look in woodworking magazines for any articles on turning. I devour anything I can find on woodturning.

The new lathe is fantastic and the saw bench is brilliant for cutting wood blanks for turning.

Victorian style spinning top with leather thong to get it going. *(Photo by Annie Dearman).*

Because the head stock swivels round it means that in theory I could turn bowls up to several feet in diameter. I love turning bowls. You secure the bowl blank to a faceplate with four screws and turn the outside of the bowl first. When it's the shape you want you start to hollow out the inside with a bowl-turning gouge. You have to make sure you leave enough wood so the gouge doesn't make contact with the screws.

Elm is a particularly good and traditional wood for bowl turning but I've used all kinds of wood including mahogany, ash and beech. It's extremely satisfying to create a bowl from a solid chunk of wood.

Before long the quality of my work is good enough for me to think about selling it. I've also built up a good range of products – spice

One of my spice racks. I usually used elm for the shelves and cherry or deal for the other parts. This one seems to be all deal. *(Photo by Annie Dearman).*

racks, ornamental eggs, dibbers for the garden, bowls, spinning tops and many other things. When they're all arranged together they look really beautiful with all the different coloured woods.

I finish some of the things I make with linseed oil and other things I finish in beeswax or carnauba wax (a very hard wax with a brilliant shine). It's easy to wax a turned piece of wood – you hold the wax against the piece and friction melts it onto or into the wood. You then just need to hold a bit of rag against the piece to achieve a shine.

I decide to write an article for *Practical Woodworking*. One of the things I make is a spinning top which you start spinning with a piece of leather thong. I make them from various woods including cherry and beech. My friend Annie Dearman comes round to my workshop and photographs various stages of the turning of a top. She's a really good photographer and the photos turn out very well. I write an article of a few hundred words to go with the photos and submit it to the magazine. A few weeks later they write to me and tell me that they want to use the article in a future edition of *Practical Woodworking*. I'm still very proud of that two-page article, but I should have credited the photo as being by Annie Dearman – that was very remiss of me.

Elm bowls and salad servers. A commission for Dave Hatfield who used to run a shop in Leigh called *Projection*. He must have done well because he retired at about forty and moved with his family to the West Country. I think there were four small bowls. *(Photo by Annie Dearman).*

Every summer an organisation called Albion organizes wonderful fairs in East Anglia. I've been to a few and love the atmosphere. The hub of the fairs are the craft stalls but there's also great music, food, theatre groups mixing with the crowd, open fires and all sorts of interesting folk wandering about.

I decide to take my turned items to sell at one of the fairs. I've a feeling I'll do well.

I've got an old sky blue Ford Escort estate which I bought from Pete the boat builder and I pack it with my turned stuff, camping gear, a tarpaulin and anything else I think will come in useful. I've arranged to go to the fair with Annie who has home-made greetings cards to sell.

When we get there the first thing we have to do is build the stall. The organisers supply rough sawn timber for that purpose. We build a very presentable-looking stall and cover it with the tarpaulin. My car is parked beside it and we erect my tent round the back. It all takes several hours but when we're done we're delighted with the home from home we've created.

Annie Dearman, a girlfriend for a while.

Almost straight away we start to sell our wares and I soon get an idea of the things that people like the most. My ornamental eggs made from exotic hardwoods such as tulipwood and zebrawood sell really well and I decide I'm not asking enough for them so I make a mental note to ask more (at the moment I haven't got anything labelled with prices – I'll do that when I'm more sure of what I can get away with).

It's good that there's two of us because it means one can look after the stall while the other can go for a wander.

The fair is very large and very wonderful. The standard of crafts is superb and I think I hold my own when compared to the other woodturners.

The smell of wood smoke pervades the air and mixes with the aroma of food cooking. Jugglers, acrobats, musicians, theatre companies, magicians all ply their trades among the crowd. There's a weird guy called Bruce Lacey who has erected a large

Some of my ornamental eggs and tiny bowls made from yew. *(Photo by Annie Dearman).*

structure with a goat's head and all manner of strange objects. He climbs up to the top, sets something alight and performs some arcane ritual.

I'm spellbound moving round the fair. I sample food from various stalls and drink some mead. The smell of cannabis is in the air and I sit on the grass with my back to a pottery stall and watch the circus of people passing and smoke a little joint. It makes everything seem even more fantastic than it already is.

Towards the end of the day people light fires all over the place and sit round them, making music, eating and quietly chatting.

Annie and I have done pretty well with our sales and there's another two days to go yet. I'm not sure I've got enough stock but it doesn't really matter and I'm filled with confidence that I can make things that people will want to buy.

*   *   *

I first saw a psychiatrist when I was twenty (not long after the drug-induced psychosis at my sister's). I complained to the psychiatrist of depression but didn't mention the highs in between. That was because I thought to be labelled manic-depressive was pretty scary stuff and in any case the highs were creative and wonderful times. How could they be part of an illness?

As a result of withholding information I was given anti-depressants and often bipolar people do not get on well with anti-depressants. They can make the highs (and subsequently the lows) worse.

This is what happened to me and after a while I realised what was happening and stopped them completely. Anti-depressants work for some manic-depressives, but not me.

It wasn't until I was in my mid-twenties that I admitted to a psychiatrist that I had highs as well as lows and I was immediately diagnosed as manic-depressive. The stock response to such a diagnosis was (and still is) to prescribe lithium which is what happened to me.

Again, many manic-depressives get on well with lithium but for me it was a nightmare drug. It did flatten me out in a very unsatisfactory way (by giving me a constant low-grade depression) but it entirely deprived me of my creative times which I obviously found unacceptable. I just felt drugged and mildly depressed all the time.

I think I took lithium for about six months then my GP decided to wean me off it and as a result my creative highs started to return.

Over the years I've been on just about every mood stabiliser known to man (lithium, Carbemazapine. Quetiapine, Olanzapine to name a few) but always it's come back to the fact that I function best without any medication. I've suffered terribly from insomnia over the years. For me it goes hand in hand with the creative highs when my brain just won't shut down. I've often not slept at all for a couple of nights. One time I went three nights without sleep and ended up in Basildon psychiatric hospital as a result. I take a low dose (5Mg) of Olanzapine to help me sleep, along with melatonin, Zopiclone (if I need it) and Kalms tablets. Put together they usually give me at least three or four hours sleep. When I can't sleep I get up and start doing creative things (like writing this).

The list of famous creative types who have been diagnosed as being (or can be suspected as being) manic-depressive is endless and ranges over all types of creative endeavor.

Amongst singers and musicians are (or were) Lily Allen, Rosemary Clooney, Kurt Cobain, Jimi Hendrix. Ray Davies, Connie Francis, Lou Reed, Robert Schumann, Nina Simone, Frank Sinatra, Dusty Springfield, Ludwig van Beethoven, Brian Wilson and Amy Winehouse (to name a few of many).

Actors, writers and poets are frequently manic-depressive. Amongst them are (or were) Robin Williams, Russell Brand, Richard Dreyfuss, Stephen Fry, Graham Greene, Ernest Hemingway, Vivien Leigh, Marylyn Monroe and Edgar Allen Poe (again, to name only a few).

A few others are (or were) Vincent van Gogh, Francis Ford Coppola, Paul Gascoigne, Mel Gibson … and hundreds of others. I'm in very good company.

It's such a strange complaint. Something that can make you virtually incapable of doing anything useful or essential and filling your soul with black treacle for a spell then suddenly finding yourself with boundless energy when you may be capable of achieving all sorts of wonderful things.

But it must be remembered that most manic-depressive types are not artists or creative people.

If I look back on my life through all the terrible spells of depression when at times I have been close to suicide, then through all the creative times when I have produced all kinds of remarkable things, on balance I'm glad I'm the way I am. It's been a roller coaster of a ride but I'd rather that than a mediochre, grey existence with no glorious creative highs.

*   *   *

I end up selling most of my stock at Barsham Fayre and almost as soon as I get home I set to work making more stuff. I design and make a kind of maze turned from cherry (all fruitwoods are good for turning) for use with my Victorian spinning tops. The idea is that you start the top spinning in an outside channel of the maze, then through tipping the top while it's still spinning you gradually move it towards the hole in the middle of the maze. It's quite difficult to reach the central hole before the top stops spinning.

A plant stand I made for Annie's mum. Cherrywood. *(Photo by Annie Dearman).*

A yew spinning top (on a piece of yew) *(Photo by Annie Dearman).*

I also design and make some small boxes with lids. I use mostly exotic timbers for the smaller items, although I also use laburnum which, along with yew (flame orange and white), is one of my favourite woods to turn. I got the laburnum from my friend Ian's tree in his Westcliff garden. He cut down the tree and I came away with lots of fat branches for turning. I'm leaving some of them to season under cover outside but some I'll use wet. They may shrink and crack a bit as they dry but that can make the turned objects more interesting.

Cherry quoits and olive ash egg. *(Photo by Annie Dearman).*

Walnut picture frames and kitchen roll holders. *(Photo by Annie Dearman).*

I'm also working on a chess set. Most of the pieces can be turned but some (such as the knights) need to be partly carved. I'm using holly (which is white) and mahogany (deep reddish brown) for the contrasting pieces.

Cherry and elm spice rack. *(Photo by Annie Dearman).*

Beech and walnut mirrors and elm bowls and platters. *(Photo by Annie Dearnman).*

I went to London the other day and visited Covent Garden craft market. I saw the guy in charge and showed him some of my work. He was very impressed with the standard and said I can have a stall there on Saturdays and Sundays. Another reason for getting up early and working on new stock.

Beech platters, olive ash egg with stand. *(Photo by Annie Dearman).*

Laminated elm bowl.

Last week I went to Norwich to a timber yard that specialises in English hardwoods (such as oak, elm, yew and ash) and exotic, beautifully-coloured timbers. I spent quite a lot of money and loaded up my Ford Escort estate and its roof rack with lots of boards, some two inches thick, some one inch.

Today I've been cutting up some of the boards into turning blanks.

I've noticed that every timber has its own smell which is released when you cut away wood with the turning tools. For instance, teak has a lovely sweet smell and oak is also sweet but slightly more pungent.

* * *

It's not surprising that so many well-known creative people have been diagnosed as manic-depressive. The energy that arrives with the mania (as long as it's relatively mild) is very special indeed and can often be put to good creative use. Some of the most brilliant people who ever lived have been manic-depressive.

Some people suffer terribly with mania when it just keeps getting higher and higher and leads them into all kinds of undesirable and at times frightening behaviour. If mania gets out of hand then often the only answer is to hospitalise that person and medicate them until they come down. Severe mania is disabling and scary. The person will lose touch with reality (i.e. become psychotic) and start exhibiting all kinds of bizarre behaviour.

One of the things manic people do is spend money like it's going out of fashion. A manic person with a credit card is not a good combination. Manic people will carry on spending even though they get themselves into serious financial trouble. I know what that feeling is like because I get it myself (but thankfully not too seriously). You get it in your head that you *must* have things. It becomes really urgent to buy those things (even though you don't need them and can't afford them). Sometimes you don't just buy one of something but perhaps four or six or more of them. You get it in your head that you're going to need them in the future so you might as well buy them all at once.

Plenty of seriously manic people get themselves into serious financial trouble because of their reckless spending.

Apart from that, dangerously manic people can upset people all over the place (and spend half their lives apologising), get into fights, don't eat or sleep for days and rush around behaving very bizarrely. They are also likely to become paranoid. For some people the mania is worse than the depression.

Fortunately I've hardly ever been seriously manic – my mania brings with it my creativity and I'm able to channel it into writing or the visual arts.

My advice to anyone who realises they have a spell of mania coming on would be to do everything they possibly can to minimize its progression and effects.

I have a regime I put into practice as soon as I realise I'm becoming manic (even though my manias are relatively mild there is still the potential for me to become too high if I don't nip it in the bud).

What I do is the following:-

- I avoid smoky atmospheres (especially cannabis smoke).
- I avoid solvent fumes of any kind (e.g. fast-setting glues or oil-based paint fumes). If fumes are unavoidable I wear an effective respirator mask.
- If possible I cycle rather than walk. It's then possible to move away quickly from difficult situations.
- Creative writing can turn excessive energy to good use. It doesn't matter what you write – just write anything and see what comes out.
- For me, creative visual work can also help bleed off excessive, unwanted energy.
- Two fresh *Kalms* tablets three times a day with meals help me no end. They can help keep you grounded and help you sleep (but use the blister pack ones – the bottled ones go off quickly once opened).
- Gentle music can help calm you.
- Breathing deeply is good.
- Staying in a quiet and familiar environment is good.
- Not watching or listening to too much news can be good. Too much news only makes you anxious.
- It's best to avoid crowded places where there is a lot of visual stimulation.
- Taking sleeping medication can help. Lack of sleep tends to make mania worse.
- I always completely cut out caffeine. I stop drinking coffee and only drink decaffeinated tea.
- I drink lots of fresh orange juice. The sugar in it helps to quell brain activity. Good quality freshly-squeezed juice if far more effective than the cheaper stuff.
- It's not a bad idea to cut up (or at least give to someone else for safekeeping) any credit cards you have – then at least you won't get into serious financial trouble.

*   *   *

I love spending time in my woodturning workshop. The lathe bench and floor soon become inches deep in wood shavings. I've a paraffin stove with a domed filament that glows red. The workshop is warm, cozy and completely rainproof.

My first chess set is almost finished and I'm very pleased with it. The problem is though that it took such a long time to make and I won't be able to ask anything like a reasonable sum of money for it. I'll make another one and see if I can do it more quickly.

Apart from the chess set I have a fair number of ornamental eggs, bowls, dibbers, spice racks, spinning tops, little boxes, kitchen roll holders and various other items that I can take to Covent Garden craft market next weekend.

*   *   *

For me depression has always been the killer. There are only two good things I can think to say about it – firstly it always ends and secondly (for me) it always leads to a creative high.

The depression itself is always a nightmare and sucks me dry of enjoyment and energy. It never becomes any easier to deal with and I spend pretty much all the time slumped in a chair watching television which gives me the illusion that I'm doing something. I once wrote a book called *Black Dogs and Blue Skies* (available through *Amazon*) which was filled with advice for people who suffer from depression but I have to say I find my own advice difficult to follow. In theory though some of the following should help if a spell of depression is coming on:-

- Making an appointment to see a counsellor (one you get on with).
- Phoning or texting a friend who understands and telling them how you feel.
- Looking at a list of your achievements in life (a list you made when you felt well).
- Looking through a photo album of your family and friends.
- Getting some good food in.
- Listening to some quiet music.
- Getting some exercise and fresh air.
- Cancelling or postponing commitments.
- Letting your mind and body rest.

- Each day doing something you normally really enjoy.
- Trying to remember the good things people have said about you, not just the bad.
- If things get so bad that you even lose the ability to ask for help, writing down the way you feel and giving it to your partner or a friend or your doctor. It could start a ball rolling in a useful direction.

*   *   *

It's Saturday and Covent Garden craft market is in full swing. I was up at five to pack the car.

I'm using a goat hair blanket I bought in Turkey to cover the stall. It's got black, brown and cream stripes and looks good under all the wooden things.

The range of crafts here is astonishing. Batik lampshades, glass objects, greetings cards, jewellery, screen printed clothing, turned items are some of the things here for sale but one of my favourite stalls is the one opposite mine run by a young husband and wife team selling all kinds of leather items. Key fobs, belts, book marks, even leather goblets, but what interests me the most is their beautiful leather chess or drafts boards. I had a word with them earlier and they've agreed to displaying one of my chess sets on one of their boards and they've let me have a board so I can do the same on my stall. There's been quite a lot of interest in the handmade chess set on the handmade board but as yet no sale. Might have to reduce the price.

Someone told me earlier that this craft market is really unpredictable. It's mostly passing trade from foreigners and some weeks it's good and some weeks it's bad. I've sold a few things today but only really enough to cover the petrol and something to eat. This won't do. I think next weekend I'll bring some lights to illuminate my stall. There's an electric socket I can use so I might as well. It could make a difference. Quite a few of the stallholders illuminate their stalls.

*   *   *

My second visit to Covent Garden craft market proves somewhat more lucrative than the previous weekend but I still don't make all that much. I'm not sure if the improvement is due to my new spotlight set-up (which improves the look of the stall considerably) or it's just a better week for no particular reason.

I get the leather workers to keep an eye on my stall while I go for a bit of a wander to look at another woodturning stall to see what he's selling and maybe to get some ideas. The other woodturning stall has a distinctly industrial look about it and I wouldn't be surprised if the things he's selling were produced on an automatic lathe. His items don't interest me that much and my stall at least looks like a *proper* craft stall with all the well thought out designs and beautiful colours of the different woods. The guy does have some rather nice pepper grinders though and I put that on my mental list of things to make. I know there's a couple of companies that sell the metal grinding mechanisms. I shall have to look into that.

A lot of his stuff just doesn't look very appealing but he may well sell quite a lot because his prices seem pretty cheap. Automatic lathes are capable of turning things out really quickly and therefore you can sell them quite cheaply. I don't want to go down that road though – for me much of the craft is in the selection of timbers and the careful turning and finishing of objects.

I shall carry on in much the same way but maybe introduce a couple of new items.

* * *

The weeks and months roll past and I manage to make some sort of living from selling my turned items but in truth I'm making barely enough to survive and I'm constantly aware that if my car should pack up I wouldn't be able to afford to have it fixed.

I go to all the East Anglian fairs I can manage but never make much money. The problem is that in order to keep your prices down and make any money at all you have to make lots of the same thing so you get quick at it and it becomes a kind of production line.

I'm much more interested in the one-off things I make like the beautiful little boxes, bowls and ornamental eggs made from exotic timbers but I can't ask a price for them that recompenses me reasonably for my labour. It's a problem and one I can't see a solution to.

In the end my car does break down (an expensive engine failure) and I simply haven't got the money to get it repaired. As a result I can't get to Covent Garden or any more of the East Anglian fairs. It's a great shame but can't be helped really and my only solution now is to sign on as unemployed.

*   *   *

Eric's finest hour occurs one day at Ramuz Drive. One day I get in and find a pile of yellow feathers and a couple of feet on the front room floor. The rest of next door's canary I guess is inside Eric. I go in the kitchen and a very self-satisfied Eric is sitting on the central heating boiler washing himself.

I am extremely proud of him this time with his new found liking for exotic pets.

I'd noticed him sitting outside the neighbor's French windows just looking in. No doubt he employed the same modus operandi to release the canary as he used to get JJ the gerbil out of his cage.

I don't see any need to tell the neighbors that my cat has eaten their canary. They must have discovered an empty cage with a canary-shaped hole in the bars.

*   *   *

Ramuz Drive is a great place to live. We have parties there but they are more civilised than the Woodfield Road ones. Our guests each bring a dish they've cooked and something to drink. We play good music on the stereo, smoke a few joints and enjoy the food and drink.

One day I see an advert for hop picking in Kent. I ring the number and arrange to drive down there the following Sunday to start picking hops on the Monday morning.

When I arrive the farmer takes me into an old cottage and shows me where I'll be sleeping upstairs. There are two beds in a small bedroom and on one of them a man of about thirty is sitting cross-legged and seems unaware of our presence, like he is in some sort of a trance. It's a bit spooky. I follow the farmer down to the kitchen and when he's gone make myself a cup of coffee.

Later that evening I go to a pub down the road for a couple of pints of beer and when I get back to the cottage I go straight to bed. The strange man appears to be asleep.

Within a few minutes of getting into bed I felt a powerful, unpleasant force somehow trying to enter my solar plexus. It was like nothing I'd ever felt before and seemed to be emanating from the guy on the other bed.

The feeling got stronger and stronger and I really felt as though it was trying to possess me.

There were no curtains on the window and when my eyes had become accustomed to the dark I could see a dim red light from a nearby oast house.

The bad feeling seemed to reach a maximum pitch and as it did so the light switch by the door started buzzing loudly and a poster on the wall of a young blonde girl in a pink dress started flapping violently.

The man started arching his back and dropping back to the bed with a quick rhythm. It was terrifying. He sat up, turned to me and said "Just let it happen". I had no intention of doing that and used every ounce of my psychic energy to resist whatever was trying to possess me. I whispered the Lord's Prayer again and again and it seemed to just keep the force at bay.

This went on for maybe an hour or so and then quite suddenly subsided and I fell into a deep sleep.

The following day when I went downstairs the weird guy was in the kitchen and I told him that worrying things had been happening the previous night. He very calmly told me that it was nothing to be afraid of and he often became a channel for dark energy when he was asleep and there was nothing he could do about it. I got the feeling he was quite proud of the fact. He went on to say that every evening at a pre-arranged time he was able to project himself to the teepee in Wales he shared with his girlfriend and would appear to her as though he was actually there. Talk about creepy. A cold shiver ran down my spine when he said that.

The weather was atrocious that Monday and unsuitable for picking hops. I lay on my bed most of the day reading.

That evening I went to the same pub for a couple of pints of beer.

When I got back to the cottage the weird guy was in bed. Almost as soon as I was in bed the same thing started happening again. I got up, got dressed and drove my car back to Southend. As I left the cottage it felt like the bad force was trying to pursue me but the further away I got the less was its power.

For years afterwards I would wake at exactly three am with the same (but more diluted) feeling that I had at the hop-picking place as though some evil force was trying to possess me.

*   *   *

One day Martin and I, who are real soul mates, did an experiment in thought transference. He sat at one end of the house and concentrated on various geometric shapes one at a time (I didn't know what shapes he was using) and I sat at the other end and tried to receive what he was transmitting. It was uncanny. Every shape he sent I was able to receive and draw. We tried it the other way round with me transmitting but it didn't work.

*   *   *

The months and years roll by. The spells of depression and creative mania come and go.

My sister Tina had a part-time job at the Palace Theatre in Westcliff. She helped with scenery-making, working directly for Zophia, the brilliant Polish set designer.

One time Tina wasn't able to go to work and asked me if I'd be interested in helping out at the theatre for a few days. That appealed to me immensely and I turned up one morning at ten for work.

The theatre had been closed for some weeks while an extension was being built. The grand re-opening was just around the corner and the musical *Cabaret* was scheduled to run for several weeks.

I helped out with scenery-making and painting and they asked me if I'd be interested in operating the flies – that involves letting down and pulling out sometimes large pieces of scenery as and when they're required or not on the stage. It sounded interesting to me so I said I'd give it a go.

I followed the stage manager up a vertical ladder which took us to an area above the stage. The idea is that the stage manager gives you your cue and you pull ropes to fly in or fly out pieces of scenery. Bits of tape around the ropes mark where you need to stop pulling because the scenery has either reached the stage or flown out of sight of the audience.

It was fascinating and I soon learnt what to do. The hardest thing was letting the curtain down so that it gently stopped falling just as it reached the stage without crumpling into an untidy heap.

I ended up seeing *Cabaret* numerous times from over the stage but not once from the audience's point of view!

*   *   *

I've seen many psychiatrists over the years. Most of them worse than useless but occasionally a good one would come along. I think psychiatry attracts the wrong sort of people because from what I gather most psychiatric doctors see psychiatry as a fast way to a consultancy and a very good income indeed. If you're only in it for the money then you're not going to be a very good psychiatrist.

I saw several psychiatrists before anyone thought to ask me if I had highs as well as lows. You would think that would be a pretty basic question to ask a patient who presented with depression, but no, they must have all been money-grabbers the ones I saw in my early to mid-twenties, then a psychiatrist at Southend Hospital (I was there as an outpatient) asked me if I ever got high as well as low and I immediately said I did.

Unfortunately the stock response then (and now) was to prescribe lithium carbonate, a drug which really didn't agree with me, and in those days (the late 1970's) they used to prescribe really high doses. Psychiatrists, in my experience, are all too fond of over-prescribing. I think it's because they are so used to medicating hospital inpatients (who usually do need high doses) that they can't get out of the habit with outpatients.

I've been over-prescribed so many drugs over the years – antidepressants as well as antipsychotics and mood stabilisers. These days if I'm prescribed something new I automatically take half or less of what I've been given because I don't want to become a non-functioning drug user.

For nearly forty years my big problem was insomnia (my maternal grandmother Olive Bell suffered dreadfully from insomnia too and took barbiturates), but not all the time – only when I was on my creative highs. It was only a few years ago when I was in my early sixties that a rather brilliant psychiatrist called Doctor Lewis prescribed a low dose of an antipsychotic called Olanzapine to help me sleep (for some reason higher doses don't help you sleep at all). It worked (and still works) wonders for me, especially if I take it in combination with melatonin (which is produced naturally by the brain to make us sleep) and if I need it, Zopiclone (a muscle relaxant that makes you sleepy). If I take that lot (plus a few Kalms tablets thrown in for good measure) then I generally sleep at least four or five hours, which is fine for me.

When I'm depressed I don't get the same problems with insomnia and generally sleep too much (and often find it extremely difficult getting out of bed at all).

I only ever had one psychiatrist who was against prescribing drugs unless absolutely necessary. He was a Swedish man who went by the name of Doctor Lars Davidsson. Another very brilliant man.

Most psychiatrists grew into doctors with the belief that drugs are king and should be prescribed whenever possible. Psychiatry is a drug-heavy occupation. Doctor Davidsson however went against that kind of thinking and delighted in *not* giving his patients drugs (apart from the ones who couldn't do without them for various reasons). For him talking was just as important, if not more so than drug therapy. He was a great believer in talking therapies and would steer his patients in that direction.

I've also had numerous counsellors over the years and on balance I would say that counselling has been of much more use to me than drug therapy which tends to mask or hide the underlying problems.

I had a fantastic counsellor called Birgit Ewald (as you may guess, a German lady). She spoke perfect Queen's English, better than most English people). I saw Birgit pretty well weekly for some five years and always benefited from my trips to Rayleigh to see her.

I've got a good private counsellor at the moment called Simon Uskuri (who is a part-time actor) who practices person-centred counselling where the counsellor is no more important than the client – both are on an equal footing.

Some kind of magic can and does happen during counselling sessions. You wouldn't necessarily think that two people talking in a room together for fifty minutes might result in beneficial things happening but it often does.

*   *   *

In the end after a few years Simon sold his house in Ramuz Drive (my sister had already moved out and moved on to another partner, Dick) and moved to a great little house in Leigh-on-Sea just up from the River Thames.

Martin moved in with Vanessa and I moved with Eric the cat to a bedsit with a kitchen and shared bathroom in Finchley Road, Westcliff.

It was the first time I'd lived on my own and I soon got to like it very much.

While I was living in Finchley Road (opposite the synagogue) I signed up for the Foundation Course in Art and Design at Southend College which I loved from day one. I was in my early thirties at the time and the majority of the students were eighteen year olds, straight from 'A' Levels.

Walk of Life (watercolour)

Watercolour flowers

It was a great course and designed to prepare students for Art and Design degree courses.

You studied a lot of subjects in not much depth with the idea of finding out your strengths and weaknesses. Subjects included life drawing, painting, printmaking, fashion design, graphics, sculpture and art history as far as I can remember.

Magical Place (watercolour)

I really enjoyed fashion design. Our project was to make an article of clothing and decorate it with aspects of a painting by a famous artist. I chose to make a *gelaba* (a male Arab item of clothing resembling a dress) and decorate it with a simplified Henri Rousseau painting with orange trees and monkeys. I used a pale blue sheet to make the garment and spent hours knocking it up on my mum's sewing machine. It was very badly made but nonetheless quite presentable.

Pauline wearing a silky top.

Somewhere there are photos of me and my girlfriend of the time Pauline wearing it in her bedroom but I can't find them. Pauline and I went out with each other for many years.

The climax of the project was when we had a fashion show to display our garments. It was great fun.

Grandpa's shirt (pastels)

Magical dancer (watercolour)

The final term was when you specialised in what you were good at (for me that was painting). It was a bit of a rush for most people what with applying for degree courses and going for interviews at art schools, but for me it was quite relaxed because I wasn't interested in applying for a fine art degree.

Paint volcano (watercolour)

Old man with red (watercolour)

*   *   *

Before long Tina had set up a studio pottery in one of the workshops under their flat. Tina made all manner of wonderful things and often went to craft fairs to sell her wares.

Ultimately Tina, Dick and Tanya moved to the West Country. Tina worked for the Western Daily Press. One of her jobs there was to colour in the cartoons. After that she worked at the Bristol Folk House where she taught art for many years and then got a job in their office.

Tanya met Gary Filer in the Somerset village where they both lived.

The Filer family and back of their dog Betsy.

They went on to get married and have three children – Shannon, Beccy and Livy. As I write this Shannon is nineteen, Beccy eighteen and Livy thirteen. Three great girls. Shannon is at Cardiff University studying International Biology, Beccy is doing a beauty course and Livy is into everything. I think Livy will surprise us all one day and do something amazing. The Filer's house is a very happy home and I love visiting them and enjoying Gary's wonderful cooking

(l to r) Shannon, Livy, Beccy. Tanya may well have taken this photo.

I moved into the same flat where Tina, Dick and Tanya had lived and spent a few happy years there. At the time I was still doing the Art and Design Foundation Year at Southend College and loving it.

Front of Betsy the Dog. Looks pretty much like the back.

137

Tanya and me.

My next door neighbors were Graham and Dot Watkins. (Dot died recently). Graham had his car workshop in Tower Court Mews, the same road that the flats were in.

Graham Watkins is an amazing guy. He was a brilliant mechanic (more of an engineer really) and able to solve any problem with any car. Graham had very long hair which he kept under a woollen hat when he was working. He employed a guy called Harry to work with him. The two of them never got on all that well and as time went on their relationship deteriorated.

Graham Watkins welding an old van of mine (which was stolen with all my hand tools soon after).

In the end Graham left the garage business and did a degree in land management at Writtle College near Chelmsford. He passed with flying colours and for a while worked for a gardening and tree surgery company.

Graham dealing with a stone sculpture in his workshop (which was stolen from his garden some time later).

When he retired Graham got into selling books on eBay in a big way and after that he started collecting Russian pocket watches. He has a beautiful little cabinet on his wall full of them.

Graham is one of my greatest friends and I often call in to see him, often to ask his advice. He's extremely knowledgeable about all manner of things.

In the end the landlords sold a large block of land, including our flats, for redevelopment and I moved to my present flat which is owned by the same landlords. Graham held out until the developers paid him enough money to encourage him to move from his home and business.

*   *   *

After I completed the Foundation Year some really undesirable young men moved into the house where I stayed in Finchley Road. They frequently got high on solvent fumes and ran amok around the house causing damage. I was quite scared of them because people who are high like that are unpredictable and can become violent. One of them had an air pistol which he delighted in using round the house.

I was still smoking a fair bit of cannabis at the time and their behaviour made me nervous and paranoid.

One day the guy with the gun shot a hole in the front door glass of my bedsit and the pellet embedded itself in the wardrobe.

It was all I could bear and I packed some things in a rucksack and left the accommodation by the back door which led to a fire escape into the back garden. I was out of there like a shot and made for the house of a guy I'd met at the college (another mature student) because he'd told me that if ever I was in need of somewhere to live he'd be able to put me up in his house in Chelmsford Avenue.

When I arrived there he was less than welcoming but when I reminded him of what he'd promised he reluctantly let me in and showed me into a small bedroom and said I could stay there rent-free.

I was so glad to get out of the Finchley Road place but my mind was working overtime and I was very manic and paranoid.

A couple of days later my sister's partner Dick took me round to Finchley Road in his van and we collected all my stuff and took it to Chelmsford Avenue. Eric the cat was dead by then – I'd had him put to sleep because he was suffering from cancer of the lymph glands.

My mind was getting really out of control because I wasn't sleeping and all sorts of strange supernatural things started happening in the middle of the night as I was visited by evil spirits (or so it seemed to me).

After a few weeks at Chelmsford Avenue I hired a van and took all my possessions round to my mum's flat in Burnham Road in Leigh. My mum had said I could stay there for as long as I liked. I put all my stuff in her large hall.

After a few nights there I got it in my head that I had to escape and late one night I left my mum's flat and ran towards Old Leigh seafront. I was pretty crackers at the time and thinking that cats were relaying messages about me to the underworld.

I tried to sleep under a boat in Old Leigh without success. I emerged from under the boat and started running towards Southend. I noticed that whenever I stopped running my thoughts and traffic would speed up like crazy so I kept on running all over town.

When dawn was just about breaking (this was February) I arrived at Chalkwell Beach and knew that when two fingers of cloud touched there would be a nuclear explosion and the world would end. My only escape was to walk to Australia under the sea.

I'd already shed my coat, tobacco tin, keys and wallet over various garden walls. I took off my jumper and walked into the sea and just kept walking out until the water was up to my neck.

A few minutes later everything went grey and I lost consciousness because of the extremely cold water.

The next thing I knew I was in an ambulance wrapped in a silver foil blanket. I learned later that a man had swum out to rescue me.

At the hospital they warmed me up and stuck a thermometer up my bottom.

When I told them I had been trying to walk to Australia they said I might need some psychiatric treatment and arranged for a psychiatrist to pay me a visit.

I was taken off to Rochford Hospital psychiatric wing and spent a dreadful couple of weeks on Southchurch Ward where I was accused of all sorts of things I hadn't done.

As soon as I got there they took a urine sample and then a while later informed me that I'd been abusing cocaine, Methodone and barbiturates which was nonsense – I'd never taken any of those drugs in my life. I tried protesting, saying there must be something wrong with their drug-testing procedure but they were having none of it. The machine was right, the machine was always right.

Every day I was there they took at least one urine sample and each day they came to me brandishing drug machine printouts and accusing me of continuing to abuse drugs while I was in hospital. It was preposterous and the accusations didn't exactly help my recovery.

I did my best to settle into the ward but it was difficult in the circumstances.

After I'd been on the ward for a day or so a man of about my age (I would have been thirty-four at the time) was admitted for treatment for severe depression. He was a tall, slender, ginger-haired man and his name was Robert Cole. Robert and I got on really well immediately and became lifelong friends.

Robert is a very brilliant poet and lives these days in France with his partner Sue.

A while ago Robert had a stroke and spent several months in a Brittany hospital. I haven't seen him since then and hope the stroke hasn't affected his poetry and poetic prose writing ability.

Robert Cole when he was still fairly slim.

He believed me when I told him I hadn't taken any of those drugs and was at a loss to explain why the results were coming up positive.

Robert in more recent years.

Robert when he and Sue lived in Colchester.

I enjoyed the food at the hospital and the art therapy sessions where you could paint what you wanted. I used to do abstract pictures using the poster paints they had on offer and tried to make them behave like watercolours. Sometimes a little group of patients would form around me and watch me painting. They were lovely people. One woman told me my pictures were like paintings of colourful tropical birds.

Just before two weeks on the ward was up I was summoned to the consultant's office and she told me that if I wouldn't admit to taking the drugs that were still showing up positive then there was nothing they could do to help me and I would be discharged. I wouldn't admit to something I hadn't done so the following day I was ejected from the hospital with no offer of any follow up treatment whatsoever. I was still very ill.

Pauline who I was going out with at the time took pity on me and said I was welcome to stay at her house until I could find some accommodation. I didn't want to go and live with my mum again so I jumped at the chance of living with Pauline for a while.

A few months after I moved in with Pauline, my sister, her daughter and partner Dick decided to move permanently to the West Country. In doing so they vacated their rented flat in Tower Court Mews, Westcliff and I was able to move in there. It was perfect for me – a one bedroom flat with easy parking outside and a nice little garden round the back.

Pauline and I were beginning to get on each other's nerves and it was time to move out of her house so the flat came up at just the right time.

Within a few days I had hired a van, picked up all my stuff from my mum's hall and installed myself in my new flat. It felt great to be living on my own again but I was grateful to Pauline for having given me somewhere to live for a few months when I really needed it. In all, Pauline and I were together for I think something like nine years. It was always a very loose relationship and that's why it worked so well for so long. Pauline was understanding about my spells of depression (which used to last usually for a couple of months or so). At such times I'd hibernate in my flat until the bad times had passed. She used to say I reminded her of a tortoise who disappeared into his shell every so often then would emerge and do all sorts of wonderful things before retiring back into his shell again.

As soon as I was in the flat I started painting again and produced many abstract watercolours which were representations of my feelings and emotions. I found it a good way to bleed off powerful feelings. The paintings were cathartic and made me feel calmer.

Abstract watercolour 1

A few feet from where I'm sitting now are two of those watercolours. I think they've stood the test of time rather well. I've had them on various walls now for over thirty years. One of them I

Abstract watercolour 2

used on the cover of this book. Vi, a friend of my mum's (both now long dead), used to love that picture and said she thought it looked like the back of the head and shoulders of an elegant woman with an exotic hairstyle. I can see what she meant but it wasn't intended that way. Us humans are very good at seeing familiar things in abstract shapes such as clouds or non-representational arrangements of colour. It makes us feel more comfortable to try and make out things we recognise.

* * *

I was extremely angry about my treatment (or lack of it) in the psychiatric hospital and I was determined to find out what had happened.

I sought some counselling and saw a lovely lady called Robbie Holloway who coincidentally had been a nursing sister at the same hospital. She resolved to find out what she could and within a few weeks she told me it looked as though errors had been made and the drug machine was giving false positives.

After that I tried to sue the health authority for medical negligence. The case went on for a couple of years but in the end my barrister decided that he would not be able to prove in court that the hospital had, by their actions, made me more ill than I already was.

I wrote a book about the whole affair (which is not generally available at present). I called it *Haunted Beach* but should have called it *The Drug Machine.* Maybe in the future I'll re-publish it under that title.

My solicitor employed an eminent biochemist who worked at the Maudsley Hospital to provide an expert's opinion. His report was completely damning of the hospital practices in relation to the EMIT drug testing machine. The biochemist had actually been involved in training people to use similar machines. He had access to all the drug test print-outs (which later on mysteriously went missing).

The good to come out of the whole sorry affair was that the hospital changed its practices with regard to operation of the machine (the operators hadn't been trained properly in how to use it and were making all kinds of errors).

At least patients who came after me would have accurate drug testing done.

*   *   *

Living on my own in my new flat worked wonders for my artistic output. I gradually got together enough work for my first solo exhibition in Southend Central Library which ran from Monday June 22nd to Saturday July 11th 1987. I called the exhibition *Songs of Colour.* It was an exciting event.

The pictures were mostly, but not entirely, abstract water colours. I also exhibited a few sculptures including one which was an abstraction of three waves and another which was a representational naked young female figure who was sitting on the floor, one hand supporting her. It was what I'd made in the evening class in sculpture at Southend Technical College (as it then was) run by Bill Freeth.

Nude study. Pen.

Self-portrait (pencil and watercolour).

At the time I was working as a computer operator for Customs and Excise and for me the sculpture course was a wonderful antidote to that.

Bull's head abstract. Poster paint.

Abstract dancing form. Watercolour.

The local press quoted me as saying, *"I'm much more interested in getting the paintings seen and appreciated by people than in selling them. It would be nice to sell things but I like having them around."* I also said, *"I think of the pictures as being pieces of visual music. I think also of birdsong, which doesn't actually depict*

Abstract watercolour 3.

anything but is just sound for its own sake. A lot of these paintings are colour for their own sake. Very often the colour itself is the subject."

I still feel the same about selling my work and I actively discourage it. Some artists measure the validity of their work by the amount they sell. I've always thought that to be a flawed equation – a work of art could be bought by an idiot who has no appreciation of artistic excellence at all and selling it says nothing about the quality of the piece.

However I did sell one thing from the exhibition – the sculpture of the female form as mentioned above. It was shiny and black and cast in resin mixed with powdered soapstone. It was pictured in the *Evening Echo* with me standing beside it and some of the paintings in the background, which could be why the guy bought it. I still regret having sold that sculpture. I used to love having it around.

I don't like selling works of art but I love giving them away to people whom I know will appreciate them.

Watercolour nude.

I left a comments book so people could write what they thought about the exhibition. Some of the comments are:-

"Keep singing your songs, David"

"Really beautiful use of colour and shape."

"The dark, moody and vibrant colours could be magnificent on a larger scale."

"I wish you had given the prices – you might have had fewer comments and more cash if you had!"

"Inspiring and imaginative,"

"First time I've ever got a strong feeling from abstract work."

"An exhibition of this kind under no circumstances should be attempted again."

"Some of the best watercolours I've ever seen. Keep up the good work."

Male nude. Pen, watercolour and gouache.

Thames Estuary, moonlight (watercolour).

"Number 11 was gorgeous. I wanted to nick it ….. it's the most enjoyable exhibition I've been to this year and I felt sure your heart was in your work and I'm pretty tired of seeing pretentious intellectual rubbish – this was a relief. You are discovering things. Keep looking."

Robert Cole towards the light. White chalk.

"It makes a change to see talent in this library."

and my favourite comment of all:-

"Art shouldn't be sold as a commodity. Give them away to friends and lovers."

Exhibiting my work and reading the comments made me feel good and gave me confidence in what I was doing. I felt like a proper artist for the first time.

In 1989 I had a second solo exhibition at the same library. I called it *A World Apart* and it reflected my concerns about human abuse of our planet.

The pictures were mostly large oils, acrylics or collages. In one picture, a large, circular collage, I used toilet paper and cocoa amongst other things (including paint). Someone commented that he hoped the toilet paper was recycled! I called that painting *Everything Under the Sun* from a Pink Floyd song.

If I ever get to heaven (for Peter Green). Watercolour.

The exhibition included one of the best watercolours I've ever done. I called it *Light* (also known as Abstract watercolour 2) and if all goes to plan with this book there should be a photo of it somewhere. There is.

Everything Under the Sun. Mixed media.

Some of the pictures were nearly five feet high (or five feet in diameter) and several of them seem to have found a permanent home behind my wardrobe.

"Everything Under the Sun" I paired with *"Ebbing Life"* and *"Climate Control Centre for the World"* I paired with *"Vanishing Forest."* Hopefully there will be photos of these paintings in this book so you can see what I'm talking about.

As with the first exhibition I sold just one thing – a watercolour self-portrait bought by my old friend John who now lives with his wife Paula in Fulking (you have to be careful how you say that) near Brighton. I'm glad he bought it because I know where it lives. The frame I made for it broke a few years ago and John had the cheek to complain to me about it! As far as I know John hasn't yet got it re-framed. I reckon a handmade frame surviving twenty-five years or so and numerous moves isn't bad going.

Ebbing Life. Mixed media.

I've had a similar experience with several other people I've given a painting or print to – they've just put them on a bookshelf or hidden them away somewhere. I see that as being unfair on me – the least someone can do having been given a free work of art is to get it framed and put it on a wall.

*　　　　　　　　*　　　　　　　　*

I loved my flat in Tower Court Mews where I lived for nearly three years. I only moved out because the landlords sold a big rectangle of land which included several buildings and my flat and the flat next door, the workshops underneath and my friend Graham's car workshop. As I said before, Graham stayed there until he was offered money to move out.

Climate Control Centre for the World. Oil.

While in that flat I started a painting and decorating business (just me) and did that for many years.

I bought a yellow van from a car auction at Chelmsford which turned out to be a real dog of a van and Graham had to do a huge amount of welding to make it roadworthy. He replaced both sills (inner and outer) and half the floor. One night quite soon after he'd

Vanishing Forest. Acrylic and oil.

done all the work I got in from work and there was nowhere to park outside the flats so I left the van with all my hand tools in it in Westcliff Parade overlooking the cliffs. By the morning it had gone. I had to buy new hand tools so I could carry on working.

Graham and his wife Dot lived in the flat next door to mine (my kitchen was adjacent to their living room).

Blue World. Acrylic.

Dot had a younger brother (I can't remember his name) who worked as a roofer. One day he had a terrible accident. He was on the roof of a two storey Post Office building and they were using a hoist to haul materials up to the roof. The hoist cable broke and wrapped itself around his leg and threw him off the roof. He landed face down in the road below. He was very severely injured (especially his face) and ended up with a big scar right across his face. The accident affected him very badly in a psychological way and one day he was visiting his elderly mother in Southend and he went berserk in the kitchen and in front of his mother he stabbed himself in the heart and died. He thought it was the end of he world. For him it was.

Later on I bought his old white Daihatsu van from Dot. It was a great little van and got me out of trouble after having had my yellow one stolen. It had a small three cylinder engine and was okay around the town but useless on motorways. Just not powerful enough.

When I was at the Tower Court Mews flat I also had a gold Ford Capri at one point. That was a great car – sleek and powerful. One weekend I replaced the camshaft – I used to be pretty handy at fixing cars and motorbikes and never got anything done in a garage. These days I get everything done at the garage.

The painting and decorating work was okay and I used to advertise in the Southend Yellow Advertiser for work. People often asked me to do other work as well and I ended up doing a lot of carpentry work for people which I loved. I hated decorating and still do.

One of my customers was a local GP who lived in a big house in Thames Drive in Leigh-on-Sea. It had been his mum and dad's house and after his father died his mum moved into a flat in Tower Court (a fifteen storey tower block) so her son and his new Israeli wife could move into the house.

Over the years I decorated every room in that house as well as the outside. The good doctor always wanted each room to be papered with the same anaglypta wallpaper and painted the same shade of yellow (the colour was a *Johnstone's* colour and it was called Parchment. I remember it well!)

The doctor said that his wife suffered from depression and the idea was to cheer her up by painting the interior of the house yellow. In all I decorated the lounge, the front room, the downstairs loo, the hall, stairs and landing, the kitchen, the bathroom and the three bedrooms. When he asked me to paint the outside of the house I was half expecting him to say he wanted it yellow but he decided on a more traditional black and white, much to my relief.

Eventually they had two extra rooms built in the loft space and I decorated them too – that time though they wanted magnolia rather than the usual yellow. Perhaps his wife put her foot down.

I once did some work for a very strange man who lived in Crescent Road, Leigh-on-Sea. He was out all day working. He left me tea-making equipment in the kitchen – each day two tea bags and just enough milk for two cups of tea. He left a tiny amount of sugar in a little bowl.

When I was working on the outside of the front bay window I got a bit of a shock when I saw a figure in the lounge seated in an armchair. It was very realistic but turned out, he told me later, to be an effigy of "Smith", the man who had run off with his wife. Perhaps he gave Smith a good kicking from time to time. He was a very strange man indeed and I hope his wife was happier with Smith.

Another job I had was to paint two rooms in an old farmhouse on the A127 (the main arterial road into Southend from London). The owner wanted both rooms to be painted with white gloss – ceilings, woodwork and walls because that was how it had always been done in the past. I'd never done rooms entirely in gloss paint before and after I'd finished I vowed never to do so again. It hadn't occurred to me but when you have that amount of surface area evaporating gloss paint it can make you quite ill. Gloss paint contains very nasty solvents which make the paint dry and if you are breathing them in all day they can make you feel pretty rotten. I had a terrible headache and felt sick for several days while I was doing that job.

*   *   *

Back in the 1980's I started going to art classes. One of the first ones was with a teacher called Carol Shillingford who held classes in watercolour and drawing at her house in Southend. I used to love going there (my sister Tina used to go as well) and it sparked in me a real interest in visual art.

Round the same time I started going to life drawing classes at Southend Technical College with a teacher called Les Shaw and loved them too. The thing I didn't like about Les Shaw's teaching was that he tended to draw on your drawing to demonstrate something. I don't think art teachers should do that..

I also went to a life drawing class at St Martin's College of Art for a year. That was fantastic and we often had two or three models at the same time. It was a very special place to study art.

Two figures Walking (Painted at St Martin's). Acrylic.

I decided to study 'A' Level Art under Carol Shillingford's guidance but I failed the exam because I didn't answer the questions properly. However, when I sat the exam a young girl sculptor whose work I really admired whispered to me that the picture I was working on was really beautiful. In truth that meant more to me than passing the 'A' Level.

Man Wading trough Water Painted in the 'A' Level. Watercolour. I love this little picture but the examiner didn't.

*   *   *

In 1989 I moved to my present flat where I've been for the last twenty-eight years. I live on the second floor opposite the War Memorial in Clifftown Parade. Each of the four rooms of my flat faces south, overlooking the Thames estuary. There are no buildings on the other side of the road and I have a clear view across the estuary to Kent. I can see Southend Pier (the longest pleasure pier in the world at one and a third miles) and both sun rises and sunsets from my flat. It's a very quiet building comprising six flats.

About twenty five years ago I took over looking after a wide border in the front garden (which had been severely neglected for many years). I still look after the border and fill it with bedding plants such as wallflowers, sweet Williams, violas, cyclamen and pansies. I recently planted a winter flowering camellia in a big blue pot which is just about to flower (it's now early October). The flowers will be deep pink. I also planted a miniature flowering cherry and its white blossom is in full bloom. It's beautiful.

Full moon over the Thames Estuary. A view from my flat. Watercolour.

I love this flat. It consists of four rooms – the living room and bedroom being at each end of the building and are mirror images of each other. In between are the kitchen and bathroom (which used to be one room which must have been split in two when the original house was converted into flats in the 1950's).

My living room and bedroom are large rooms and in a corner of the bedroom I have a printing press for printmaking which I bought off eBay for £1600. It's probably worth well over £2000 now. That sort of equipment holds its value well.

In the living room I have a woodburning stove which I installed a couple of years back. I had to employ a roofer to finish off the steel pipe which goes up to the chimney pot. He also fitted a cowl to stop wind affecting the stove and to keep the rain out. I love lighting the stove in the winter and burn mostly logs with a bit of coal. Before this stove I had a pot belly one for about twenty years which I used so much that in the end I wore it out. The present stove is all legal with a council safety certificate and a carbon monoxide alarm.

Way back in time there was a well-known local jeweller and benefactor called R.A. Jones who used to have a shop with a big clock outside in Southend High Street (less than ten minutes walk from my flat). It's said that he and his family used to live in Imperial Manor which is where I live now. The house was built about 1890 and the top floor (my flat is at the front of the top floor) has two balconies with the original art nouveau railings. Where I live would have been part of the servant's quarters I imagine they took up the whole of the top floor).

I once went in the basement of this building and there is still the original cast iron central heating boiler with ash from its last fire still in it. That boiler would have run on coal and supplied those big old cast iron radiators that were popular in times gone by. I assume the old boiler was installed when the house was built.

The stairs up to my flat are narrow and steep. That could be a problem in future because I have developed a lung disease called pulmonary fibrosis which causes me to get short of breath. I have to pause after the first flight of stairs before tackling the final flight up to my flat. However, the landlords have said that should I need it I can have a stairlift installed for the final flight of stairs. I probably will need one in the future.

Three or so years ago I had an emergency one night when I couldn't breathe properly and had pains in my chest, arms and back. I rang 111 and was told an ambulance was on its way. A few minutes later an ambulance arrived with blue light flashing. The paramedics came up to my flat and hooked me up to a defibrillator to check out my heart which they discovered to be ok. A few minutes later a second ambulance crew arrived and told me they were the emergency crew. All the paramedics knew each other and once they'd found there was no emergency we all relaxed and had a tea party in my living room!

The chief paramedic was very interested in my medication and when I told him I'd been on a massive daily dose (80Mg) of *Simvastatin* he said that could be the cause of my lung problems. He wrote out a report and told me to show it to my GP as soon as possible. I didn't sleep at all that night because of all the excitement and was at my GP's by nine o'clock the following morning. I showed her the report (it happened to be the same doctor who had prescribed me the statin in the first place) and she told me to stop taking the drug immediately. She also said she suspected that I had pulmonary fibrosis, which turned out to be true. When I looked at the patient information leaflet for *Simvastatin* it said in very rare cases the drug could cause interstitial lung disease, and pulmonary fibrosis is a type of that.

I made an official complaint about my GP's because I was (and am) of the opinion that they should have monitored me with regard to taking *Simvastatin.* I was on the drug for six and a half years and not once was I reviewed. I should have been reviewed every year. I think statins are very dangerous drugs but the drug companies are reluctant to admit that because statins are the biggest money-making drug *ever.*

Statins are very useful for very many people but the same effect can be achieved through diet and exercise.

*   *   *

Way back in the 1960's my maternal grandparents used to enter the Beecroft Open Exhibition and on several occasions had one or more of their lovely paintings accepted and exhibited. I don't know if they sold any.

In the 1990's I started entering the same exhibition and over the years I have had several paintings and prints exhibited. I always have them "not for sale" because as I explained above I don't like selling works of art. I prefer to hang them on my walls at home or give them away. At present on my living room walls I have forty-five paintings, prints and photographs and in the bedroom another fourteen. My walls would look very bare without them.

The Beecroft Art Gallery began I think in the 1940's. The building (near what was to become the Cliffs Pavilion) was bequeathed by a Mr Beecroft, although it has seen better days and is now propped up by huge pieces of timber.

Several years ago the Southend Central Library (where I had my solo art exhibitions) closed as a library and became the new home for the Beecroft Art Gallery. They normally have several exhibitions on at any one time. I went there a couple of weeks ago and saw a fine exhibition of huge photographs by a man who is almost blind and can only see things as if through a tunnel (tunnel vision). At the same time on the first floor there was a wonderful picture representing all the ships and aircraft (including Amy Johnson and her plane – only the tailplane was ever discovered) that have ever gone down in the Thames estuary. The picture must be four or five feet square and is done in dark brown ink. Each sunken ship, pleasure craft, aeroplane or Zeppelin has its own little image. There must be over a hundred in total.

*   *   *

1996/7 were busy years for me. In 1996 I did the Foundation Year in Art and Design (for the second time) at Southend College. I enjoyed it so much the first time that I decided to do it again. Not with the idea of applying for a Fine Art degree like most of the students but just for fun.

The second time I did the Foundation Year I specialized in sculpture under the excellent tutelage of Dave Taylor, a fine

A two-headed Celtic style wooden statue, one head looking to the future, the other looking to the past.

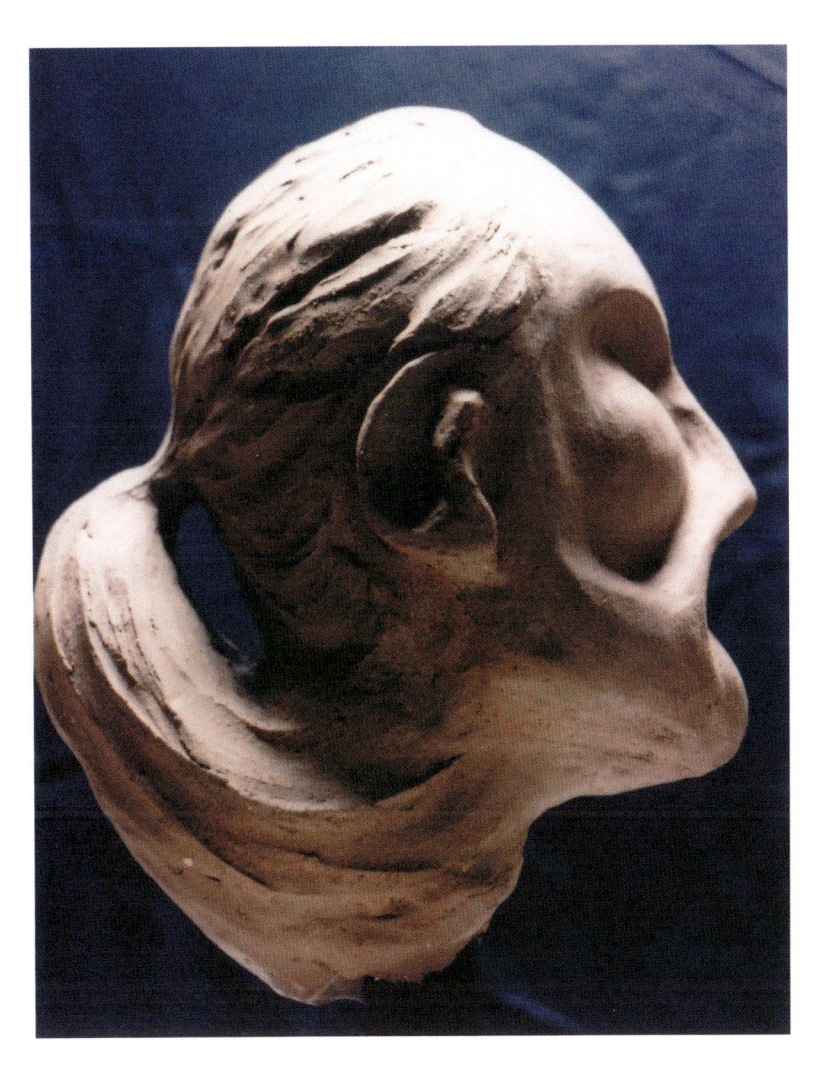

Male clay head.

sculptor and teacher. At the time he was fresh out of university and twenty-two years old. He was full of enthusiasm and ability.

I made quite a few sculptures on the course. The only ones I have now are a black resin head which is full of sand and lies heavily on its side and a metre high long, thin sculpture which represents an ancient Celtic figure with two heads – one looking to the past, the other towards the future.

Female dancer with fabric.

Dave Taylor himself no longer does much in the way of teaching but has his own workshop where he practices his art.

In Southend there is a park called Priory Park. In the past the imposing main entrance gates had a bronze lion seated on the top of each of the pillars supporting the massive gates. Many years ago under cover of night the lions were stolen (presumably to be melted down). Dave was given the commission to make two replacement lions for the pillars. He made them from fibreglass and resin and they now stand proudly on top of the pillars. He finished them with bronze powder and from the pavement they look as though they've been cast in bronze. If anyone tries to steal them they will get a surprise when they discover them to be made of worthless fibreglass!

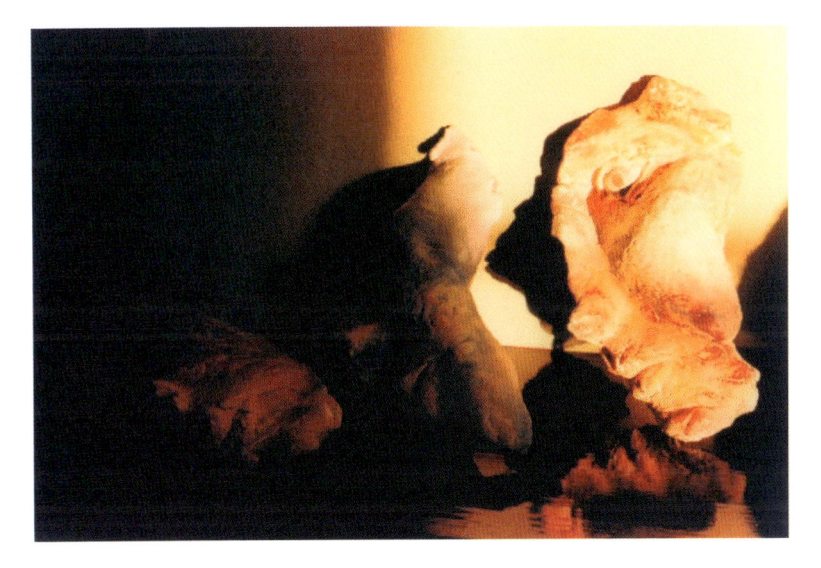

Three waking heads.

There's a great fish and chip shop in Westclifff called *Oldham's* and another of Dave's commissions was to make a six foot long cod to protrude at a right angle from over the shop. He painted it gold and it looks fantastic. He also made the cod from fibreglass and resin.

Another of his commissions was to make a huge model of a *Star Wars* spaceship which looks as though it has crashed into empty retail units at one of the Southend shopping precincts.

Female clay head.

I love spending time watching Dave in his workshop. He's able to chat while he's working and he's fascinating to watch.

Also in 1996/7 I was busy working on the radio dramas that were accepted for production and broadcast by RTE Radio 1 in Dublin (RTE is Ireland's BBC). In all they used four of my plays:- *The Flight of Huxley*, *The Holy Chicken*, *Stanley's Blues* and *A Decent Pair of Skyhooks*. I went to the recordings of *The Flight of Huxley* and *A Decent Pair of Skyhooks*. RTE paid for me to fly to Dublin and back but for some quirky reason would not pay for my accommodation. I didn't have much money at the time and on each visit I stayed in a cheap Dublin hostel.

Attending the recordings was quite an experience. The first one I went to was *The Flight of Huxley* (which was a comedy about a man, Huxley, who decided to break with the habit of a lifetime and much to his wife's horror went out one Wednesday morning and had all sorts of weird and wonderful adventures. At one point he is allowed to experience flying like a kestrel). In truth the radio people prefer the author not to be there for the recording. Once you've handed over the script to them they consider it their property and don't want the author interfering in any way. I was very good. I sat quietly and only spoke when spoken to. I met the actors, the producer and the sound people and the whole experience was interesting and fascinating. At the time they had a huge reel to reel recording machine through which the master tape moved very quickly (for quality of sound). These days I expect they achieve the same thing digitally.

It worked like this. The actors would read through a few pages of my script then when everyone was happy to go ahead they would record those pages and the master tape would be stopped while they went through the same process again. Gradually the play would come together on the master tape. It took a day to record a half hour play.

In the gallery with the producer and myself was the sound guy whose job it was to insert sounds from CD's or tapes. In my play *The Flight of Huxley* I had instructed that there be some 'bluesy saxophone music' and the sound guy had got a friend of his to record a piece of sax music specially for the play.

The other sound guy was on the floor with the actors and we could see them through the big gallery window. His job was for instance to open or close doors or make the sound of footsteps approaching or receding.

It was incredible how everyone worked together on my script and made a living, breathing play out of it.

When *The Flight of Huxley* was in the can the producer (a lovely man called Brendan O'Duill) took me to a pub and I got very drunk on Guinness. So drunk that he had to put me on a bus and instruct the driver to stop and let me off when we reached my hostel!

When I attended the recording of *A Decent Pair of Skyhooks* Brendan didn't take me out to get drunk.

Having plays broadcast on the radio is a strange experience. You write a play, send it off to the broadcasting people, if you're lucky it's accepted, you perhaps attend the recording and eventually the play is broadcast. You get absolutely no feedback at all. The play goes out and is heard by I guess hundreds of thousands of people but you never know if any of them enjoyed listening or if any of them hated your work. It's very strange, that silence.

*   *   *

From late 1996 to late summer 1997 was when I attended Birmingham University to do an MA in Playwriting Studies which was run and taught by the playwright David Edgar. I got on the course on the strength of my radio drama work.

To start with there were thirteen students on the course but after a while one of them dropped out. We had to attend the university on Mondays and Tuesdays for lectures, workshops and tutorials. The rest of the week was when we were supposed to work on our essays and projects. As well as three six thousand word essays we each had to write a full length (i.e. two hour) stage play. The course was intensive and fun and we had some good visiting playwrights including Terry Johnson and Tom Stoppard.

I was driving an old green Ford Fiesta at the time. It wasn't the most reliable of cars and had done a high mileage but surprisingly it didn't let me down at all and survived numerous trips to Birmingham and back.

At the end of the first Tuesday I drove back to Southend and by the Friday I wasn't well at all. I had a pain across my belly which got worse when I eat something. On the Friday evening I went to visit my mum in Leigh. She realised I wasn't well and said I could stay the night in her spare room.

By about half past midnight I realised I wasn't at all well and I called the emergency doctor. He turned up a few minutes later, stuck his finger up my bottom and said he suspected appendicitis. He called an ambulance which arrived a few minutes later and I was sped off to Southend General Hospital.

The pain in my belly was by then excruciating and on arrival at the hospital they gave me plenty of morphine which didn't help much. They kept increasing the dose until it was effective.

I had an emergency laparotomy operation (where they make an incision to investigate the problem) and they discovered that my appendix had ruptured.

The following morning as I came round from the operation it seemed to me that all the voices I could hear were Australian ones. I lay there with my eyes shut trying to work out how I had come to be in an Australian hospital.

Eventually the voices became non-Australian and I opened my eyes to find myself in a ward near the nurse's station. A nurse came up to me and told me I'd been so desperately ill the previous night that they all thought they were going to lose me.

I had all kinds of tubes – an operation drain, a catheter, a tube up my nose into my stomach, and a drip in each arm. I also had an oxygen mask over my face.

At one point a doctor came down the ward to visit a man opposite who was having kidney dialysis. I distinctly heard the doctor say to the patient, "The best thing you can do mate is smoke as much as possible." That was just what I wanted to hear (which I guess is why I imagined it). I'd had the presence of mind to bring my tobacco, cigarette papers and lighter with me to the hospital and someone had put them in the bedside cabinet. I just about managed to turn over and get them out of the cabinet. I rolled a cigarette, put the oxygen mask on top of my head and lit the cigarette. I'd had quite a few puffs before a stern female voice shouted, "Who's smoking?" A male nurse came to me, grabbed my cigarette and threw it out the window. "You can't do that in here, mate", he said.

The combination of high fever, anaesthetic and morphine was making my mind play tricks. That night some strange things happened. I could see a bank of TV screens at the foot of my bed and each was playing a different rock band. Also, on my bedside cabinet was a get well card with a little dog on it and I saw and heard the dog turn to me and start barking.

I was in hospital for two weeks and spent the next month or so recovering. Eventually I felt well enough to return to the MA course. I'd missed half the first term and they all said they were surprised to see me back, thinking I'd probably put off my return till the following year, but I was determined to catch up and did in the end.

On the course I wrote a play which I called *Trapping Birds* about a father and son who lived in a crumbling stately home. The father wanted his son to marry, have a son of his own and take over the running of the house but the son had different ideas and wanted to spend his life as a sculptor, using artifacts from the house to make his creations. There was a huge amount of tension in the play between father and son.

At the end of the course each student had the first hour of his or her play professionally directed and staged in the university's theatre. The plays were put on over a weekend in front of an invited audience of friends, relatives, agents and theatre professionals. For me the most difficult aspect of the whole course was having to sit on the stage facing the audience and trying to answer questions about the play that were thrown at you by the audience.

I passed my MA in Playwriting Studies and I'm quite proud of that considering that I had some nasty spells of depression during that year and I missed half the first term.

*   *   *

Round about the year 2000 I went on a week long dance photography course run by the wonderful movement photographer

Hilary Shedel. The course was run at Central St Martin's College of Art in London and there were maybe ten students. Each day we had at least one professional dancer to photograph. It was a brilliant course and I came away with hundreds of photos of dancers in motion. I still use them today as inspiration for prints.

* * *

Paul Newell in his house in New South Wales.

In early 2001 I visited Australia for the first time. My friend Paul Newell (the guy I went hitch-hiking with to Greece when we were both eighteen or nineteen) lives near a little place called Billinudgel in New South Wales, about a twenty minute drive from Byron Bay on the east coast. The area where he lives is very green and usually gets flooded in their Autumn (our Spring). I went there in February and the weather was mostly sunny but sometimes very rainy. Their valley got flooded when I was there and we were housebound for several days.

Paul on his ride-on mower.

I love Australia. It's nothing like I imagined it to be. I must have formed my expectations from watching *Neighbors* and *Home and Away* which give a very distorted idea of the country.

The first time I went Paul was still married to Diana, a yoga teacher. They have since divorced and his partner now is called Camille.

Paul's house is single storey and usually has some small snakes living in the gutters. When I was there there was a big python inhabiting the rolled-up garage door. One evening Diana went to the garage to get something and surprised the python which had caught a rat and had dislocated its jaws in order to swallow it. Diana said the snake was as surprised as she was!

Where Paul lives is a popular cannabis-growing area and frequently police helicopters circle overhead looking for signs of the crop growing in the wild (people often cultivate cannabis away from their homes so they don't get caught). If they find cannabis growing they land the helicopter and destroy the crop.

I looked at the map, saw a place called Lightning Ridge and decided to hire a car from Byron Bay and drive there. It was quite an adventure. On the map Lightning Ridge (which is also in New South Wales) didn't appear to be that far away from Byron Bay but Australia is a vast, vast country and it took me several days driving to get there. After that I bought large scale maps so at least it looked as though I was making some progress.

Paul leant me a tent and on the way I stopped at a place called Die Hard Creek and set up camp. The drive to the rudimentary campsite was down a long, steep track which was lined with wallabies perching on the rocks.

After I'd set up camp a middle-aged couple arrived in their camper van and invited me over to share their camp fire and beer. I spent the evening with them. The man worked for Telstra, Australia's British Telecom, and he was an engineer responsible for a huge area which took him a day to drive from one side to the other.

Before I joined their camp I needed some milk and ended up driving a round trip of ninety miles to get it from the nearest shop. Distances in Australia are ridiculous.

I eventually arrived at Lightning Ridge and wasn't disappointed. It's a mining town producing some of the finest black opals in the world. The term black opal is a misnomer because the opals are beautifully and brightly coloured and anything but black. I'm not sure why they call them black opals.

Opal fields waste dump near Lightning Ridge.

Lightning Ridge has a real Wild West feel about it. It's said that the dodgy-looking men who drive their big 4X4's with ferocious-looking dogs sat beside them all have guns in their glove compartments. Huge amounts of cash change hands there and it's not surprising the guys are very protective towards their money.

In shop windows I saw adverts for prostitutes who visited the town for two or three days at a time and I imagine made a lot of money.

At Lightning Ridge I stayed in an old Sydney tram with a malfunctioning and extremely noisy air conditioner. Temperatures reached well over forty Celsius and I put up with the high temperatures because the accommodation was so cheap.

Early one morning I drove seventy kilometres or so along a red dirt track to visit an opal workings waste dump. Every few minutes a lorry would arrive and dump some more soil and rock. As soon as the lorry stared unloading people would gather around the back of it searching for opals in the spoil. The mines have no running water and the spoil is taken unwashed to the dump. It's not unusual to find lovely opals amongst the waste. I had a good search but had to leave about eleven in the morning because it got too hot to bare. I found a few bits and pieces but nothing to write home about.

When I left lightning Ridge I went back a different way and ended up doing a big circle back to Paul's place. On the way I stayed for one night with the Telstra engineer and his wife at their house in the coastal town of Grafton. On the way to and from Lightning Ridge I had driven along several red dirt tracks and the underside of the car had become coated in red dust. One of the conditions of hire was that the hire company would make a surcharge if there was evidence of having driven on red dirt roads. The Telstra engineer gave the underside of the car a good hosing down to destroy the evidence so I wouldn't have to pay the surcharge.

On the flight back from Australia in 2001 I had one of the best experiences of my life. It was dark outside and the cabin crew were encouraging people to get some sleep by giving out blankets and pulling down the window shutters. The last thing I felt like doing was sleeping and I asked one of the female flight attendants if I could visit the flight deck and have a chat to the Captain. In those days you could do that. She said she'd give him a ring and ask him if he wanted to entertain a visitor. A few minutes later she returned and told me it was my lucky night and the Captain and his second in command would be happy to see me. My seat was near the back of the plane and she led me to the front, up the stairs, through the first-class area and into the flight deck itself. The plane was a 747 Jumbo jet and it was fantastic in there. I remember red and blue lights everywhere and the fact that the Captain and his mate weren't even looking out of the cockpit window. I commented on this and they said they came into their own on take-off and landing. The Captain said if I looked out of the side window I'd be able to see the lights of the city of Lucknow in northern India and sure enough the city was illuminated in all its beauty below. He also said that the white light rapidly approaching us was the light of another 747 a thousand feet above us. It was astonishing how quickly that light reached us and went overhead. The Captain said the combined speed of the two aircraft was well over a thousand miles an hour.

I must have been chatting to the Captain and his mate for twenty minutes or so before the flight attendant arrived to escort me back to my set.

I'm so glad I visited the flight deck that day – now (because of the twin towers terrorist attack later that year) it's not possible to do that any more. In the past it was common for people to visit the flight deck of big airliners. I feel really privileged that I was able to do that.

A couple of years after my first visit in 2001 I re-visited Australia and had all sorts of adventures again. That time I flew to Perth in Western Australia and stayed with Paul's friends for a few days. I hired a car and drove to Kalgoorlie, one of the old gold mining areas of Australia. There was a gold rush there in the late nineteenth century (I think it was mainly comprised of Chinese men).

Alongside the highway from Perth to Kalgoorle is a big (maybe three or four feet or so diameter) metal water pipe which carries fresh water to the town. It hugs the highway all the way and is Kalgoorlie's only water supply.

Kalgoorlie is still a gold mining town and has one of the biggest open cast mines in the world. Where they've opened it up you can see from a distance tiny black dots in the rock. Each dot is and old mine shaft.

One day I hired a metal detector and set off in search of gold. A woman at the hostel where I was staying demonstrated the sound for gold I needed to listen out for. I spent a few hours detecting in intense heat but didn't find any gold.

Quite close to Kalgoolie is a small place called Ora Banda. Someone in the hostel told me it would be an interesting place for me to visit but wouldn't say why. He said he'd tell me the story when I got back. I set off fro Ora Banda in my hire car and found my way to the pub I'd been told to visit. I had a beer in there then returned to the hostel. The guy who had suggested I go there then told me about the recent history of the place.

The pub at one time had been run by an ex-policeman and was a very popular haunt for bikees (in Australia motorcyclists are called bikees rather than bikers). The ex-policeman decided to try and attract a different class of customer to the pub and banned the bikees from the pub. The bikees took exception to this and one night one of them arrived at the pub and planted a large bomb against one of the pub walls. The explosion killed the ex-policeman and severely damaged the pub. The moral of this story is don't mess with Australian bikees as they can be quite evil.

Opposite the hostel where I was staying in Kalgoorlie was a brothel. It was strictly illegal but tolerated nonetheless. One day I took the ten dollar tour. There must have been about half a dozen of us on the tour. We crossed an open courtyard and some of the girls were sitting round a big table drinking coffee and chatting. They watched us pass with a mixture of amusement and contempt. Inside the brothel we were shown some of the specialist rooms. I remember an ancient Egyptian themed room and a medical room with all sorts of strange equipment. At the end of the tour the woman who was showing us round said we were quite welcome to make use of their services if we wanted but no-one took up her offer.

My third and final visit (so far) was I think in 2013 and I had a great time then as well. On that visit I visited Brisbane (about three hours on the coach from Byron Bay) and stayed there for ten days or so. I stayed in a sixteen storey tower block hotel just over the road from the Roma Street Transit Centre, a hub for buses and trains.

When I was a child I used to collect the cards they gave away in packets of tea and one series I collected from PG Tips packets was of Australian cities. My favourite card showed Brisbane and the river which runs through it. (the Brisbane River). I discovered when I went there that it's a very beautiful city.

It's a great city for walking round – not too big and very flat. Where I stayed was near the centre and I walked everywhere from there.

Brisbane is a great place for street art. There are anonymous grey metal boxes about four feet high in the streets (I think they are something to do with the Fire Department) and many of them have been decorated with paintings, some very elaborate.

One day I was walking towards the centre of Brisbane and I saw a life size bronze sculpture of a kangaroo sitting on a metal bench. On the pavement beside it were three baby kangaroos, also made of bronze.

I find Australia an addictive place. There's un underlying Britishness about it but in a tropical or sub-tropical context. You get parrots in the gardens, see all kinds of exotic creatures and wonderful flowers and trees you've never seen before. I'm sure I'll go back to Australia for a fourth visit one day.

*   *   *

In 2005 I published a book which I called *Black Dogs and Blue Skies*. It's a self-help book for people who suffer from depression and is full of advice about how to approach it. I like to give the book to people whom I think might appreciate a copy. It was a very satisfying project for me and I consider the book to be one of my best achievements.

The cover of my book *Black Dogs and Blue Skies*

*   *   *

Round about twelve years ago (approximately in 2005) I became involved with the mental health organisation called Rethink. At one time it was called the National Schizophrenia Fellowship but they changed the name. It's a wonderful organisation and offers help and support to anyone with a severe and long term mental illness. Bipolar disorder comes under that umbrella and I had a lot of help from them over many years.

I made two really good friends at Rethink – Simon and Alison and see each of them from time to time. Alison often comes with me to my hospital visits to the Royal Brompton Hospital in Chelsea where I go to have my lungs checked out every few months. Alison is exactly the right sort of person to have with you on a hospital visit. She's funny, positive and likes to chat. My visits to the Royal Brompton are so much more enjoyable if Alison comes with me. We always go to St Luke's church near the hospital for a coffee, a sandwich and a piece of cake. St Luke's is where Charles Dickens was married.

* * *

My Honda Hornet 600 at Buckfast Abbey.

Over the past ten or twelve years I've made many visits to Buckfast Abbey in Devon to stay with the Benedictine monks

Me in the guest lounge at Buckfast Abbey (self-portrait).

(whose habits are black) in their monastery. The grounds of Buckfast Abbey are split by the River Dart on its way to Dartmouth and at Buckfast it must be some thirty metres wide.

Detail of one of the abbey windows

A cloister at Buckfast Abbey.

An icon I painted for the monks during one of my stays at Buckfast.

I love staying at the abbey. For obvious reasons only men are allowed to stay in the monastery itself and eat with the monks in their refectory although there is accommodation within the abbey grounds for couples and single females.

Autumn trees at Buckfast Abbey.

The monastery is so quiet and peaceful. It's actually Devon's top tourist attraction and many coaches arrive each day and the people visit the church, the shops, the sensory garden and the restaurant. From inside the monastery you can't hear them or see them and you'd never know they were there.

Meals are taken in silence (which can be surprisingly noisy with the sound of cutlery and crockery) although at the mid-day meal a monk reads from a book (not normally a religious book).

Accommodation for male visitors is excellent – there are comfortable guest rooms most of which have an en suite shower room. Brother Daniel the guestmaster, whom I have got to know quite well over the years, often gives me a fantastic room overlooking a quadrangle. The room is exceptionally large with a big bed, two sofas, an armchair, a desk and a table. It's adjacent to the guest lounge where I have met many interesting people over the years. Many Catholic priests go to Buckfast on retreat and it's interesting to meet them out of their usual context. One of them once told me a joke. A man died and went to Heaven. Saint Peter greeted him and said, "You can do more or less what you want here but whatever you do don't go behind that wall." "Why's that?" the man asked to which St Peter replied, "Because that's where I keep all the Catholics and they think they're the only ones here!"

You could substitute any denomination or religion for the word Catholics.

Apart from silent meals the monks are not allowed to talk between the end of Compline (the last office of the day at about nine pm) and the following morning. If you see a monk in the cloisters with his hood up it means he is praying and is not to be disturbed.

Coffee is drunk from bowls, a tradition which goes back to the French origin of the present monastery.

The history of Buckfast is fascinating.

The monastery was founded in the year 1018 (so its millennium is this year) and thrived until Henry the Eighth dissolved all the monasteries because the Catholics wouldn't let him divorce. After that the buildings fell into disrepair and much stonework was removed for local building projects.

In 1883 (I think) a group of French monks decided to reinstate the monastery and over the next fifty or so years the monks themselves (aided by one or two professional stone masons) rebuilt the monastery and church on its original foundations. The abbey has photos of monks in their habits working on wooden scaffolding.

I hope to make many more visits to Buckfast Abbey in years to come. I've visited the abbey by train, car, van and motorbike.

Buckfast (on the edge of Dartmoor) is wonderfully situated for trips to Dartmoor, Plymouth and the Devon and Cornwall coast.

When I visit Buckfast I always call in to see Tina and her husband Andy (who plays a mean ukulele), my niece Tanya and family and

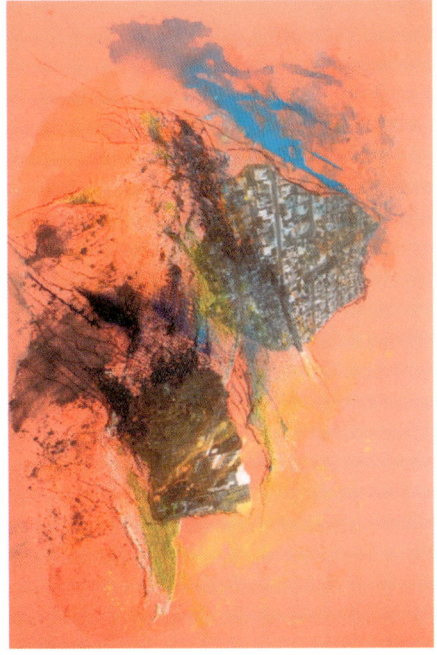

Two of Tina's pictures from her garden studio in Weston

my friends Pete and Pat in Devizes. It breaks the journey and it's lovely to see them all.

I was down at my sister's place in Weston-super-Mare just a couple of weeks ago on a flying visit to pick up some family history information. On the Sunday morning I woke up early and went for a walk on Weston beach which is very wide when the tide is out. I was walking along the prom and an elderly gent came towards me and gave me an enthusiastic greeting. I asked him if there was a toilet nearby. He said there was but I'd need a twenty pence piece for it. I said I'd come out without any money and it didn't matter, I'd just have to wait till I got back to my sister's place. "Hold on", said the man, "I normally carry a twenty pence piece in case I get caught short." He fished the coin out of his pocket and gave it to me. As it happened the toilet was locked shut so I gained twenty pence. The man was way in the distance by the time I discovered the locked toilet. What a nice, friendly thing to do for a stranger.

A bit later I was walking on the beach and kept seeing signs warning of sinking mud. A middle-aged female runner in a hi-viz jacket came towards me and panted a 'good morning' as she passed. I asked her if she could tell me about the signs for sinking mud and she told me they referred to quicksand which was not far out. She said the quicksand isn't in one area but occurs in random pockets indistinguishable from safe mud. She said that many people had died over the years when they sank without trace into the quicksand. What a horrible way to die. I imagine once you sank to chest level you'd be able to breathe out but not breathe in and you'd suffocate. Either that or the fast-moving tide would sweep over your head and drown you.

The woman told me that a father and his two children died in the quicksand some years ago.

I thanked the woman for her information and warning and she set off running again.

*   *   *

One thing I've found really beneficial over the years is massage. I've been going to the same woman, Mel, for well over twenty years. When I first met her she was in her late thirties, now she's in her early sixties. She's never lost her touch! She practices aromatherapy massage and I like a combination of lavender, ylang-ylang and maybe rosewood or frankincense.

Aromatherapist Mel with her oils.

It's a wonderful hour in the company of an expert. These days I can't smell the oils so well because I've virtually lost my sense of smell but the oils still have their effect, for instance lavender is very relaxing and can make you feel sleepy later during the day or evening.

We always have gentle music playing during the massage and I go away feeling invigorated yet relaxed.

Mel and I get on extremely well and often talk about spiritual things.

*   *   *

Hadleigh tree. Vinylcut.

In 2009 I began a course in printmaking at the Southend art college. It was a few hours in the evenings or Saturday mornings once a week. I realised straight away that it really suited me and we had a brilliant tutor (himself a very respected printmaker) called David Lintine.

The printmaking studio is a wonderful place. They have a relief press in there that was made in early Victorian times and still works well (as long as it's maintained properly). The other main press is an intaglio press (pronounced intallio) on which you can make various types of prints such as drypoint, etching or monoprints.

Miss Harding. Vinylcut.

Drypoint is where you use a very sharp metal tool to scratch a design into a metal or plastic plate. Scratching the surface of the plate raises burrs. You pass the plate through the press (which exerts huge pressure) and the ink trapped in the burrs creates the print..

Dancer against the light. Vinylcut with watercolour.

I never did any etching so I don't know much about the process.

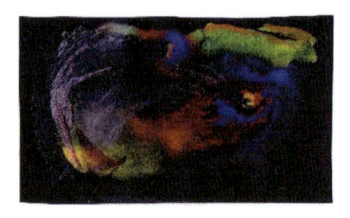

Ghost dancer. Drypoint and paint.

After Emil Nolde. Monoprint.

Monoprints are one-off prints. You ink up a plate however you want (using as much coloured ink as you like) and pass the plate through the press. Monoprints are unpredictable (which is why I like them) and often very beautiful.

Eric Bibb. Vinylcut print.

It's possible to combine various types of printmaking in one print.

I got on best with relief printing where you cut a design into a block and then print it using the relief press.

The traditional way was to use lino for cutting the design but these days vinyl is often use instead. I think the stuff I use is a heavy kind of floor covering. If you use a sharp gouge you can cut into

Cooling Towers, Scotland. Vinylcut.

vinyl as though it's butter and it has no grain, unlike lino. I just didn't get on with lino. I found it really difficult to get a flow of cuts going.

I've made many prints over the years and the great majority of them are relief prints.

Steve Weston Playing the Blues. Vinylcut.

Watercolour Dancer 1. Vinylcut.

The cut blocks are things of beauty and I never destroy them (like a traditionalist would tell you to after making a numbered edition) – I just don't make numbered editions and keep the blocks. Sometimes you have to put two fingers up at traditionalists.

It's called relief printing because everything you don't cut away prints (i.e. what's remaining stands out in relief).

The printmaking workshop is a lovely place with its presses, inks, benches and printmakers tools such as rollers and palette knives.

These days water-based inks are used in preference to the old-fashioned oil-based inks when you needed copious quantities of white spirit to clean up. These days only water is required.

Robert Cole. Drypoint.

Cleanliness and cleaning up the room after a session is essential in printmaking.

A few years ago I bought a second-hand intaglio press so I can practice the art at home.

*   *   *

Over the past twelve or so years I've made many trips abroad by motorcycle. I love going to foreign countries (on my own because then I meet many more people than if I was with others).

I tried going away once in a group of six motorcyclists but it was a disaster and everybody wanted to do something different. Besides that I didn't get on with the guy who appointed himself leader. After less than a day we split into two groups of three then the day after I went off on my own and had a great time.

Verdun, France. Moslem graves. Ossuary (bone house) tower is in the background.

On that trip I visited Verdun in eastern France where there was a huge First World War battle which cost the lives of hundreds of thousands of men.

One of the most memorable parts of the trip was visiting the ossuary (bone house) which contains bone fragments of tens of thousands of young men. The fragments were picked up from the battle fields. The ossuary is a long building with a central tower shaped like a shell. At night a light casts a cross over the surrounding cemeteries. It's a very moving place.

On the way back I visited Paris for a few days and stayed in a wonderful little hotel with a cinematic theme. The owner was a delightful man who was obsessed with all things related to film and cinema.

For the early trips I used my Honda 600 Hornet which was a fantastic bike. It was black and very rugged. You can't beat Hondas for build quality.

On another trip I went by ferry from Plymouth to Santander in northern Spain. Then rode west across the top of Spain and down the west coast and into Portugal. I ended up staying at a great little hotel in Porto for a couple of weeks or so (the manager offered me a substantial reduction if I stayed two weeks or more).

I love Porto. It's a great city for walking round – not too large and very interesting.

It's where the drink port originated and you can visit the cellars where it's stored.

I spent many happy days walking round the city and discovered a great library where they had the *Guardian*. It's a very beautiful city and I was so impressed that I went back (by bike again) a couple of years later and stayed at the same hotel.

One time on the return ferry to Plymouth the sea conditions were atrocious in the Bay of Biscay and the Captain suggested all passengers should stay in their cabins for safety. I got bored with that and kept nearly rolling off my bed and decided to make my way (by grabbing handrails all the time) to the restaurant at the top of the ship. There was another guy already there and together we sat overlooking the bow of the ship. It was fantastic. The waves

My Kawasaki Z1000 in Spain.

A roof in southern Spain (looking towards Africa).

were massive and the ship was pitching and rolling like nobody's business. Every so often a huge wave would crash into the bow and spray would go right over the top of the ship (which was, I think, ten decks high). Behind us crockery, trays and cutlery was crashing to the floor. It was very exciting.

On the same voyage one of the other motorcyclists was taken ill and the ship had to be diverted to sail close to the French coast so he could be lifted off the ship by helicopter. I don't know what happened to him or his bike.

Another time I went on a motorcycle adventure to the Irish Republic. I took the ferry from Fishguard I think to Cork and had a great time travelling round the west coast. I visited the site where Alcock and Brown crash landed their plane next to a Marconi radio station after flying from America There's a very beautiful monument shaped like an aircraft tail plane to commemorate the occasion.

The Alcock and Brown memorial, Ireland.

My final trip (so far) was a pilgrimage to visit the house of my favourite artist, Emil Nolde (pronounced Nolder – you always pronounce the final 'e' in German like you do in the word 'Porsche').

I was on my Kawasaki Z1000 which I had at the time and took the ferry from Harwich to Esbjerg in Denmark (that ferry no longer runs). On the ship I met a lovely guy who was on his way to play the organ at various Lutheran churches in Esbjerg.

I rode across Denmark to Copenhagen and stayed there a few nights. I then rode across the beautiful and magnificent Öresundsförbindelsen which starts as a tunnel in Denmark then halfway to Sweden rises out of the sea and becomes a bridge for several kilometres. It finishes at Malmö.

In Sweden I rode down to the southernmost tip to a place called Ystad (which featured heavily in a Swedish TV detective series which I can't remember the name of. All the filming was done in and around Ystad).

I stayed in a hostel that was fifty metres from the sea. The guy who ran it had bicycles for hire so you could ride on the paths through the woods to the sea.

I took the ferry from Ystad to an unpronounceable place in Poland, stayed one night there in a lorry driver's hotel which was full of smoke (the guys were even smoking while they were eating their breakfast), then rode the few miles into Germany.

I stopped at Hamburg for a few nights and met a hotel manager with Romany ancestry who told me I should try out my grandmother's crystal ball as it might work for me. He told me crystal balls find people who can see things in them and it's not always women.

After that I rode across the top of Germany to its border with Denmark and on to Emil Nolde's house. It was autumn and really after the end of the tourist season so there was no-one else there. I stayed for a few nights in one of his two houses where his parents used to live. I was the only guest in the huge farmhouse which was built on a little hill to prevent flooding. That part of Germany and Denmark is very flat and prone to flooding. The people round there have astonishingly blue eyes and their German accent is very soft.

The land and seascape near the house is bleak and beautiful.

Nolde was one of the artists persecuted by Hitler because he didn't paint cozy little family scenes that the mad dictator liked.

His house (which he had designed and built) overlooked the flat countryside and from within you could see for many miles around.

Nolde was banned by Hitler from painting (he was considered to be one of the 'degenerate artists') but you can't keep a good artist down and for the duration of the war he gave up oil painting (in case the SS officers arrived and smelt the turpentine) and painted tiny watercolours on Japanese paper. The paper was so thin (yet strong) that it is hard to tell which side has been painted on – the paint soaks right through. Nolde hid the pictures under the floor and they weren't discovered until the nineteen-sixties. I went to an exhibition of them in London many years ago and was astounded by their beauty. Each picture he started off as an abstract arrangement of colour and then painted in faces and figures that the shapes suggested to him. The paintings became known as the 'unpainted pictures' because he wasn't supposed to have painted them.

A hundred metres or so from the old farmhouse I was staying in was a fairly new restaurant (also owned by the Nolde Foundation) which employed young deaf people to be trained up as waiters, waitresses and chefs.

Again, most evenings I was the only customer. The food was superb and the trainee staff were falling over each other to serve me!

Nolde's own house is now an art gallery (as was his wish) exhibiting his pictures. He tried to convert some of the small watercolours into large oils but in my opinion that wasn't very successful.

I loved staying in his house and felt his presence was somehow still very much there. I once went to Monet's house at Giverny and felt his spirit had fled the place because of the hordes of Japanese tourists.

My next adventure may well be to take my beautiful Honda CB1000R to visit Vincent van Gogh's place at Arles in southern France. On the way there (or maybe back) perhaps I'll visit my friends Robert and Sue in Brittany.

Another small adventure I want to embark on is to visit my friends Gary and Jo on the Isle of Wight. I'll probably go on my motorbike. Gary is a brilliant musician (chiefly a sax player). who has played with many bands all over the world. His first professional job was playing with the *Rocky Horror Show*. I love to hear Gary playing. He's so incredibly inventive.

His partner Jo used to clean my flat. She's a woman of many talents and an excellent photographer.

They have fairly recently bought a camper van and they stay in it when Gary has a gig.

*   *   *

A few years ago I joined the Seawing Club at Southend Airport and took up flying lessons. They use two-seater Cessna 152's for instruction and I enjoyed it tremendously although had to give it up in the end after seventeen or so hours instruction due to the cost. One day when (if) I've some spare money I'll go back to it.

I had I think four different instructors over a couple of years. I ended up with the Chief Flying Instructor, a lovely man called Harry Page who has the perfect temperament for a flying instructor – honest and firm yet kind.

My interest in flying was sparked by a trial lesson in a yellow Tiger Moth biplane at the Imperial War Museum's site at Duxford. One of the great things about flying is that you take control of the aircraft from Day 1. If you mess it up the instructor will of course retake control.

I had a second lesson in a silver Tiger Moth at Duxford and became hooked on flying so that's why I joined the Seawing Club.

The Cessna 152 (the number relates to the wing area) is a great little plane with a very sturdy engine.

Taking off is easy – You use maximum throttle and when the aircraft reaches about seventy knots you can feel it trying to fly and you pull the control column towards you and she takes off. It's as simple as that.

Once you've climbed away from the runway you turn the plane towards the compass heading you want and adjust your height and speed according to what the instructor tells you. You might climb to 1500' or 2000' to practice level flight, climbing, descending and turning.

One time I flew over to Kent to a place called Motney Hill where we used to live before we moved to Southend when I was about six or seven. I took photos of the water treatment works where my dad used to work as a maintenance fitter and the associated houses for the workers. It was fascinating seeing it all from the air.

Another time I flew to where I now live and took photos of the war memorial and the building where my flat is.

For another lesson I flew to Duxford and the instructor landed the plane on the grass. If you fly into Duxford they let you have two hours free in the huge museum there. The instructor and I drank tea and eat cake then I took off for Southend Airport.

Motney Hill, Kent. Houses and water treatment works.

My final lesson (so far) was to fly a Cessna 172 (a four-seater) to Shoreham in Sussex. I had my friend Paul Fowkes and his son Joe in the back and our mutual friend John Hazard was there to meet us. We went off for a bacon sandwich and a coffee in a café and the instructor waited for us at the airstrip.

I took off and flew all the way back to Southend without the instructor touching the controls. That time I landed the plane myself at Southend Airport. The landing was a bit bouncy but we got down safely enough. I'm proud of the fact that I've landed a plane at Southend Airport.

Writing about this has made me want to take up flying again. I love it and would love to become competent. I'm not too bothered about getting a private pilot's license but I guess that's something to aim for. You have to be familiar with all kinds of subjects including meteorology, radio work, navigation and air law. You also have to take a number of exams but I don't think they are too daunting. Maybe one day.

         *   *   *

I've been playing blues harmonica since I was fourteen. It was my friend Pete Lee (him of the long black hair, drugs and black clothing) who first encouraged me to give it a try.

Until a few years ago I'd only ever played along to records but then I decided to form my own band and the *Rocket Blues Band* was born.

We've only ever done four gigs, one at *Chinnerys* on Southend seafront and the other three at the *Railway Hotel*.

Four gigs and three different lead guitarists.

Well that just about brings things up to date and I hope you've enjoyed reading about my life.

I hope I'll be able to stay in my flat. I hope I'll play more music. I hope I'll be able to travel and ride my beautiful motorbike for many years to come. I hope I'll be able to get down to stay with the monks at Buckfast Abbey and visit my family in Somerset and my friends in Wiltshire. I hope I'll have more flying lessons.

Who knows what the future will bring? None of us fortunately.

Printed in Great Britain
by Amazon